Velma J. L 1 th n t

BOTH-WIN MANAGEMENT

BOTH-WIN

MANAGEMENT

*A Practical Approach to
Improving Employee Performance,
Using the 8-Step
RPM* Program*

Chester L. Karrass
and William Glasser, M.D.

*Reality Performance Management

LIPPINCOTT & CROWELL, PUBLISHERS   NEW YORK

ACKNOWLEDGMENTS

We wish to acknowledge the advice, assistance, and managerial support of Doug Naylor, Director of the Educator Training Center, and Gary Karrass, Vice-President of the Center for Effective Negotiating. The entire RPM project, with its seminars, ten video tapes, audio cassettes, workbook, and this book, required a great deal of effort, logistical coordination, and encouragement from Doug and Gary and their organizations.

FIRST EDITION

Designed by C. Linda Dingler

U.S. Library of Congress Cataloging in Publication Data

Karrass, Chester Louis.
  Both-win management.
  Includes index.
  1. Supervision of employees. I. Glasser, William,
joint author. II. Title.
HF5549.K269   658.3′14   79–25656
ISBN 0–690–01809–6

---

80 81 82 83 84 10 9 8 7 6 5 4 3 2 1

This book is dedicated to our wives, Virginia Zappala Karrass and Naomi Silver Glasser, who were participants in the development of the book from its beginning and who helped us gain important insights we would not have had otherwise.

Contents

We have written this book to serve the needs of people at two levels: in business and in their personal lives. Our goal in business was to help managers and supervisors at all levels of the organization from company president to lead man deal with the hard-to-handle people and performance problems they face daily. On a personal level we wished to show that the ideas of Reality Performance Management (RPM) can help our children, our spouses, and others we love to gain the confidence and strength to live more fulfilled lives.

The Both-Win Management approach developed in an unusual way over a period of years. As friends and neighbors since 1953, we would talk about our respective specialties, one in negotiation and the other in psychiatry, counseling, and education. While our professional pathways were widely diverse, we discovered that we both shared a common goal—to help people perform better on the job and in their lives and thus to be happier—and that our methods of achieving our goal were similar.

About two years ago we developed a seminar program combining the Reality Therapy and Both-Win Negotiation techniques. Interested managers who attended were highly responsive to the RPM approach and encouraged us to write a book and put our program on video tape cassettes. Both-Win Management appealed to these executives as a sensible and workable approach to handling people and helping them improve. When we asked these same executives how they presently handled problem employees and whether what they did worked, they readily admitted that their present methods were not only failing to improve unproductive behavior but in many cases were making matters worse. RPM, with its systematic, psychologically sound eight-step program, offered a practical effective alternative.

We suggest that you begin practicing Both-Win Management tomorrow morning. Practice on your employees, on your children, on those you love and live with, and on yourself. Before long you will see those with whom you interact gain the strength and confidence to become increasingly self-responsible and self-disciplined. When they grow stronger and live more fulfilled lives, you win also.

Chester L. Karrass

December, 1979

William Glasser, M.D.

INTRODUCTION

RPM: A Radically New Approach to
Improving Manager and Employee
Performance

The first thing we do when presenting Reality Performance Management (RPM) to groups of managers or supervisors is ask them to tell us what their employees do or fail to do that causes them the most difficulty. From company president to lead man, they invariably tell us the same thing. Their problems range from employees who complain "It's not my fault" to those who fail to meet commitments; from those who do only enough to get by to those who never check their work; from those who are chronically late or absent to those who are problem drinkers. At every level, managers encounter *excuses* instead of *performance*.

The trouble with these and other recurring personnel problems is *that most managers handle them in a way that guarantees that they will grow worse.* What they do is diametrically opposite to what they ought to do. Such employee difficulties are never easy for the manager to deal with. They cause aggravation and tension for everyone concerned, yet they must be handled properly or they grow worse. Left unattended, they negatively affect not only your employee's performance but also your own performance as a manager. Dealing with these and other common management problems in a way that satisfies both you and your employee and prevents the problems from recurring is the subject of this book.

You will find that although RPM is based on valid theory, this is not a theoretical book. Its purpose is to give you a clear idea of what to do when difficulties with personnel and employee performance arise. Essential to RPM is the manager's learning to focus on the employee's inadequate behavior, behavior that is both the core of the problem and the place to start to solve the problem.

RPM does not dwell on complex psychological theory. Rather, it is based on two complementary approaches to effective management. One approach, known as Reality Therapy, holds that the most effective thing a manager can do in dealing with an employee who is performing poorly is create a warm, non-stressful environment. In such an environment the employee can feel safe to face the reality of his or her inadequate performance and, with the manager's help, take the responsibility to improve.

The second approach, known as Both-Win Negotiation, is similar in that it encourages the manager to create a situation wherein the employee feels that he or she has not only an incentive to improve but a reasonable chance of doing so—of winning. Furthermore, from the manager's point of view, if the employee wins, the boss wins as well. By doing an effective job of motivating the employee, the manager too has gained in position. They both win.

RPM combines Reality Therapy and Both-Win Negotiation to teach you skills that will help you handle successfully the broad range of employee conflicts and managerial dilemmas you encounter. You will learn how to avoid the negativity trap—spending time and effort moaning about what goes wrong rather than actively working toward positive solutions. When the RPM technique is used correctly, employees will gain the strength to handle themselves and their work in a self-responsible manner.

Employees who perform according to the RPM method use their own initiative and take responsibility for getting the job done, rather than waiting for others to tell them what to do. They are able to handle the assignments you give them, as well as more difficult assignments that involve increased challenge and responsibility. The more employees with this attitude you have working for you, the more work will be done in a pleasant, efficient way. As a manager or supervisor, you will have a lot more recognition to give employees; and, as they gain recognition for a job well done and feel a greater sense of their own worth, you will gain too.

When you are surrounded by strong, fulfilled people, everybody wins.

INTRODUCTION

WHAT IS RPM?

So much for claims. What is RPM? Basically, Reality Performance Management (RPM) is a way of working with employees that quickly gets them to direct their attention to their behavior, to what they do and think, much more than what they feel. By using the techniques of RPM, the manager learns to push employees gently toward RPM's key concept: *I am responsible for what I do.*

RPM teaches you to accomplish this goal of better employee behavior and performance through a series of eight easily learned steps, which are detailed in this book. Briefly, the steps are:

1. Establishing and keeping a good relationship with each subordinate.
2. Using that ongoing relationship to get the employee to lay on the table what he or she is or isn't doing right.
3. Asking the employee to evaluate his or her behavior in terms of its effect on the job to be done and on fellow workers.
4. Negotiating with the employee to develop a realistic, workable plan to handle the situation in a better way.
5. Getting the employee to agree to follow the plan and providing an equal commitment to help if your help is needed.
6. Asking for and accepting no excuses for why a job cannot be done better.
7. Criticizing in a constructive, not punitive, fashion.
8. Not giving up easily (the good manager is a model for the dogged belief that there is always a better way—and shows it by not giving up).

Too many managers find themselves choosing to deal with their employees through a "commonsense" form of negotiation that can never work. Simply stated, they attempt to solve the problems that arise through one-win negotiation techniques. But in a one-win negotiation, there is always a winner and a loser. This type of negotiation may be fine for a poker game, or even occasionally acceptable in a short-lived personal encounter. But when you work with people daily on a long-term basis, you must never negotiate in this way, because no matter who wins, the manager or the employee, the company is the loser, Therefore, we shall emphasize over and over that *both-win* is the only acceptable kind of negotiation between manager and employee. RPM is based on the principle that *the group can never win if any member of it loses.*

RPM is a firm and effective but human way to handle people. When you master the eight steps and incorporate the both-win technique into your relationship with your employees, you will be in a position to deal with personnel and performance problems calmly, fairly, and with good sense. When problems arise, you will no longer be tense or anxious about what to do or how to do it.

HOW MANAGERS MAKE MATTERS WORSE WHEN THINGS GO WRONG: THE "UPSIDE-DOWN" THEORY

The "Upside-Down" Theory holds that most managers or supervisors do exactly the opposite of what they should do when things go wrong. Instead of correcting the personnel and performance problems that plague them, managers often make matters worse.

When things are going smoothly and the work is being performed and getting done satisfactorily, it's easy to deal with people. Unfortunately, in the real world, such a happy state rarely lasts. All kinds of problems arise. A manager has to deal with employees who want raises but haven't earned them, with workers who pay more attention to personal business than to the jobs they were hired to do, and with people who are careless or perform only the minimum amount of work when more is necessary. As if this were not bad enough, the organization is staffed with the usual number of malcontents who gripe, goldbrick, arrive for work late, take long breaks, call in "sick," get drunk, and so on. Faced with the difficult task of trying to solve all these problems, managers frequently do exactly the opposite of what they ought to do.

Let's take Bob, for example. Bob, who has been an employee in the Acme Cabinet Company accounts receivable department for five years, is just not getting the work done. He is behind in mailing out invoices, doesn't keep up with necessary accounting entries, and allows receivables to remain unpaid for too long. But Bob performs many parts of his job reasonably well, and he knows quite a lot about Acme's customers and products.

The typical manager would first discuss the matter with Bob.

Then, if there was no improvement, the manager would nag and eventually resort to threats. If after all this time and effort there was still no improvement, the manager would then have to consider terminating Bob. If Bob could not be easily terminated or replaced, the manager, having already lost faith in Bob's ability or willingness to improve his performance, would spend less and less time with Bob except to criticize his work, complain, wheedle, and stridently demand more. For as long as Bob remained employed at Acme, the two would remain in ever-worsening conflict. This estrangement, compounding the original problem of Bob's nonproductivity, would give the manager a double headache. Not only is Bob's time being used ineffectively, but now the manager spends equally inordinate amounts of time engaged in an ineffective battle of wills.

The situation will remain deadlocked until the manager realizes that the only hope lies in establishing real communication with Bob, not in allowing barriers to be built. If we wish to motivate Bob to perform more effectively, what we have to do is get closer to him, not farther away, and use this closeness to teach him to perform better. We use this common example to show that when our employees need us most, they often tend to get us less. When we move away from them, or give up on them entirely, they grow weaker instead of gaining the strength and confidence to improve their performance.

To add to the management dilemma, when dealing with an employee who is performing badly, like Bob, managers tend to go back into the employee's past history of failure, pointing out again and again how many times the same mistake has been made. Soon, the manager is bogged down in unproductive arguments about who caused what to whom and when. These arguments allow the manager and Bob to release their emotional frustrations, but they also make it much harder to get the *facts* of Bob's present performance on the table and discuss them rationally. Once more an upside-down error has been made. If the manager doesn't focus on *performance,* to the exclusion of almost everything else, there can be little help for a troubled employee.

To aggravate the situation even more, the manager then makes the mistake of telling Bob what he must do to "straighten out," jamming a "get-well" approach down Bob's throat rather than *ne-*

gotiating with him to develop a better performance plan to which Bob can commit himself. When later Bob fails again, they get into yet another heated discussion, with Bob giving all the reasons and excuses why the job couldn't be done. Soon, in utter frustration, the manager resorts to punishment and threats to coerce Bob into improved performance. When that approach fails, as it always does, the manager gives up in despair and drifts still further from Bob, thereby ensuring that Bob's work will become even worse.

RPM differs radically from the kind of "upside-down" or "one-way" responses that most managers and supervisors give when confronted with a problem employee. Think it over. See if you haven't made most of the mistakes we've talked about. "Upside-down" responses to management problems are natural and only too human. It isn't easy to pinpoint performance and talk about it with an employee who is performing poorly. Nor is it easy to get rid of the hurt feelings and frustrations managers often have when the job is not getting done. If performance and personnel problems were easy to avoid and/or handle, more of us at every level of the company would be dealing with them in a more effective way.

Many of you reading this book will say, "Why spend so much time and effort with problem employees like Bob? If they don't shape up, fire them." We have discovered, like most managers, that it is not only wasteful to fire people but, in many cases, inappropriate to do so. Wouldn't it be better to help them perform more effectively, even if it means a 180-degree change in the way you handle your employees? Improving performance is the most powerful way there is to care for and help people.

WHY SOME PEOPLE ARE STRONG AND EFFECTIVE: THE FLYWHEEL THEORY

Central to RPM is the concept of strength, and this is best explained using the flywheel theory, which shows why some employees are strong and effective while others are not. Imagine a bicycle wheel upside down, suspended on its bearings as shown in the figure. The Flywheel Theory sees psychological strength and weakness as a moving flywheel, spinning sometimes rapidly, sometimes slow-

THE PSYCHOLOGICAL FLYWHEEL
IN EACH OF US

ly, and sometimes turning hardly at all. Every time we experience success, our flywheel spins faster. A strong, successful person has a fast-spinning flywheel that will spin for a long time. The longer this person's flywheel spins, the more momentum the flywheel has to keep on spinning. A slow or stopped flywheel, however, denotes psychological weakness. It occurs when a person's successes are few and far between, and it is a sign that the person is failing.

Between successes, the flywheel of a stronger person continues to spin. This inertial spinning can be looked at as our reserve strength, the strength we use to cope with hard times. Persons who are weak have slowly spinning flywheels and therefore have little or no reserve strength, a fact that is apparent in the way they perform.

Naturally, big successes put a lot of spin on our wheel and can keep us going for a long time. For most of us, however, life consists much more of a series of small successes that keep our wheel spinning smoothly and regularly.

Failure, on the other hand, acts like a brake. It can bring the wheel to a screeching halt and make us feel as though we can't do anything well at all. Even a small failure is felt as a perceptible loss of strength, and each failure slows the wheel down and robs us of needed reserve. A series of failures, or a long period without success, may slow our wheel to the point where we find it very difficult to get ourselves going. When you see someone survive a massive failure and keep going, you can assume that person's wheel was spinning very rapidly before the failure occurred. That's why successful managers, even those who have had periods of failure themselves, find it so difficult to understand a failing employee. After all, these managers reason, their own wheels spin through thick and thin. They find it nearly impossible to relate to a person whose wheel has stopped altogether.

As more and more success causes our wheel to spin more and more rapidly, we become aware that we are developing a reservoir of strength that we can draw on whenever necessary. Too much failure, on the other hand, slows our wheel and drains our energy reserves, undermining our confidence in ourselves. Convinced that there is nothing we can do, we attempt little or nothing. When this happens, we become immobilized, our flywheel motionless. If such a person is in charge of others, his or her lack of strength affects everyone being supervised. A general manager whose flywheel has stopped spinning can slow down or stop a whole organization.

HOW PEOPLE HANDLE HARD TIMES AND FAILURE

Whether a person is strong or weak, the effect of hard times is the same—they slow the flywheel down. As the flywheel slows, even strong people may begin to experience some self-doubts, some lack of confidence, but these doubts aren't overwhelming. These people recover because while their wheels are still spinning, they have the good sense and confidence to be creative, imaginative, and dogged enough to find some success, somewhere, to keep things going.

They never let their flywheels stop completely. Then, when times get better, they're ready to take advantage of the turnaround.

But when people feel weak and lack confidence, their slowly spinning flywheels grind to a halt when hard times come. In fact, until such times come, it may not be possible for them (or for others) to recognize their weakness; but when hard times are at hand, they quickly discover they don't have the strength to take on new challenges. They begin to avoid new tasks. They do less and less, make more excuses, and are quickly overwhelmed with feelings of personal failure. Although many weak people appear to be strong, what they do not have when all the chips are down is the strength to go ahead and do the job.

Employees like this, who have little or no reserves to draw upon, often become depressed, nervous, or physically sick in an effort to excuse their inability to perform. They hope that, because of their upset, less will be demanded of them, or even that someone will help them do things they ought to do themselves. When even this fails, they may turn to drink in a last-ditch effort to block the problem or to believe, in their falsely confident state, that their flywheels are going fine, disregarding performance to the contrary.

Conclusion

Every step of RPM is based on the assumption that we can and should help our employees keep their flywheels spinning. A stronger employee leads to a stronger company. Therefore, the bottom line of RPM is that it can be put to work on the day-to-day personnel and performance problems that every manager faces—whether lead man or company president. With reasonable effort, RPM can be used effectively at any level of the organization. Managers and supervisors who learn the Both-Win Management techniques will find themselves spending less time with problem employees and getting better results.

PART ONE

Building Employee Self-
Responsibility and Performance:
Putting the RPM Approach to Work

Part I of this book is concerned with putting the RPM—Reality Performance Management—approach to work in building employee self-responsibility, strength, and performance. We will consider the four pathways that lead employees to success and the three downhill stages that lead employees to failure.

With this as a base for understanding successful and failing employees, we will see how the eight steps of RPM can be applied to solve the wide range of problems that managers and supervisors face daily. Each step will be explained thoroughly, and easy-to-apply suggestions and techniques will be given to help you put RPM to work.

Before we go further, think about how you are presently handling problem situations and whether or not your present approach is working. Take the "How Well Do You Handle Problem Employees?" quiz that follows. There are five choices for each question. Circle the number in front of the choice that best represents your present management approach. After you have finished, you can evaluate your present managerial approach by scoring the quiz according to the directions given.

HOW WELL DO YOU HANDLE PROBLEM EMPLOYEES?

(Typical problem situations: Employees who do sloppy work, procrastinate, don't check their work, take too much time off, are late, make excuses, goof off, lack interest, or do only enough work to get by.)

1. When negotiating a plan to solve a problem with an employee, how specific regarding what is to be done and when, milestone checkpoints, and measurable results, do you tend to be?

   (1) VERY SPECIFIC (2) RATHER SPECIFIC (3) SOMEWHAT SPECIFIC
   (4) RATHER GENERAL (5) PREFER GENERAL PLAN

2. When trying to get at the facts of an employee's recurring problem or an employee's poor performance, do you find yourself listening patiently and fully to the employee's feelings, worries, anxieties, frustrations, personal problems, and problems with other employees?

   (1) RARELY (2) OCCASIONALLY (3) MODERATELY OFTEN
   (4) FREQUENTLY (5) ALMOST ALWAYS

3. How close do you get to your chronic problem employees who show no appreciable improvement?

   (1) SUPPORTIVE DAILY CONTACT (2) PLEASANT AND CORDIAL
   (3) SOMEWHAT FRIENDLY (4) INFREQUENT CONTACT (5) AVOID THEM

4. Do you have trouble getting problem subordinates to realistically evaluate the consequences of their actions in terms of themselves, the company and others they work with?

   (1) LITTLE DIFFICULTY (2) MODERATE DIFFICULTY
   (3) DIFFICULT BUT SUCCEED HALF THE TIME
   (4) CONSIDERABLE DIFFICULTY
   (5) VERY DIFFICULT, USUALLY HAVE TO EVALUATE THE SITUATION FOR THEM

5. You and your employee have negotiated a plan to solve a performance problem with detailed milestones. How often do you check to see that the employee is progressing as agreed?

   (1) ALMOST ALWAYS (2) FREQUENTLY (3) MODERATELY OFTEN
   (4) OCCASIONALLY (5) RARELY

6. Do you find yourself resorting to threats and punishment as a means to improve behavior?

   (1) RARELY (2) OCCASIONALLY (3) MODERATELY OFTEN
   (4) FREQUENTLY (5) ALMOST ALWAYS

7. When your employee fails to do a job, do you listen carefully and patiently to find out what went wrong and why in order to understand if the reasons are valid?

    (1) RARELY (2) OCCASIONALLY (3) MODERATELY OFTEN
    (4) FREQUENTLY (5) ALMOST ALWAYS

8. When discussing a problem employee's chronic behavior, do you tend to get involved in past mistakes, omissions, and associated problems?

    (1) RARELY (2) OCCASIONALLY (3) MODERATELY OFTEN
    (4) FREQUENTLY (5) ALMOST ALWAYS

9. You and your employee have negotiated a plan for better performance. How firm a commitment from the employee that he or she intends to meet the plan do you *normally* get?

    (1) VERY, VERY FIRM (2) FIRM (3) MODERATELY FIRM
    (4) SOME COMMITMENT (5) NOT MUCH COMMITMENT

10. When trying to get at the facts of a recurring problem situation or an employee's chronic unproductive or disruptive behavior, do you find yourself getting into heated emotional outbursts and arguments with the employee?

    (1) RARELY (2) OCCASIONALLY (3) MODERATELY OFTEN
    (4) FREQUENTLY (5) OVER AND OVER AGAIN

11. Do you tend to criticize and carp at your problem employees in the hope that they will get the point and improve or quit?

    (1) RARELY (2) OCCASIONALLY (3) MODERATELY OFTEN
    (4) FREQUENTLY (5) OVER AND OVER AGAIN

12. How much performance improvement do you aim for when negotiating an improvement plan with a poor performer who has many different problems?

    (1) ANY ONE SMALL IMPROVEMENT
    (2) ONE MEANINGFUL IMPROVEMENT (3) SEVERAL IMPROVEMENTS
    (4) BRING WORK LEVEL UP TO THE STANDARD OF OTHERS
    (5) URGE EMPLOYEE TO DO BETTER

Scoring

Total the circled numbers. This will give you your total point score. Now you can determine whether you fall into the high, low, or intermediate range in handling problem employees:

- If you scored between 12 and 25 points, you are probably getting good results with problem employees.
- If you scored between 26 and 43 points, your ability to handle problem employees will be improved with RPM.
- If you scored between 44 and 60 points, the RPM approach will prove extremely useful to you in handling problem subordinates.

Take the quiz again several months after reading this book. If by that time you are regularly using the RPM approach, your score will have improved, and so will your success in motivating employees to improve their attitude and performance.

In chapters 1 and 2 we will explain why some employees move toward success and others move toward poor performance. This will provide us with the framework we need to put the eight steps of RPM to effective use.

1

The Pathways to Success: How Some Employees Move Toward Success and Others Move Toward Poor Performance

In this chapter we will explain why some employees perform well and others poorly. This will help you as a manager or supervisor to understand the pathways by which employees gain the strength to improve their performance. It will also help you to understand and relate to your peers and subordinates in a different and more perceptive way.

Using the concepts of success identity and failure identity, we will explain what makes some employees strong and effective while others are weak and ineffective and also what the differences are between these two groups. Throughout our explanation we constantly refer to the chart titled "The Basic Concepts of Reality Therapy" that follows. Somewhere on this chart you will find yourself and everyone you know. We suggest that you keep this chart in mind as you read this chapter and the next one.

SUCCESS OR FAILURE—WHICH WAY?

As you can see, the chart is divided into two halves. The right half is titled Success Identity; the left half, Failure Identity. This represents, basically, how the people of the world are divided, with a majority on the success side but a substantial minority who view themselves as failures.

We believe that built into each of us is a need to continually monitor the way our life is going. As complex as this total ongoing evaluation may be, we constantly reduce it to a simple summary

THE BASIC CONCEPTS

FAILURE IDENTITY
LONELY—Less Rational
Little or Nothing to Look Forward To

WEAKNESS ◄——————————

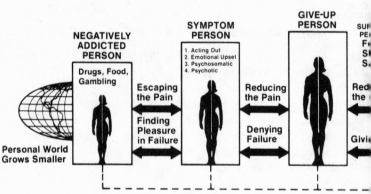

NEGATIVELY
ADDICTED
PERSON

Drugs, Food,
Gambling

Personal World
Grows Smaller

Escaping
the Pain

Finding
Pleasure
in Failure

SYMPTOM
PERSON

1. Acting Out
2. Emotional Upset
3. Psychosomatic
4. Psychotic

Reducing
the Pain

Denying
Failure

GIVE-UP
PERSON

SU
PE
F
SI
S

Red
the

Givi

POSITIVE ADDICTION (ONE HOUR A DAY ALTERNA

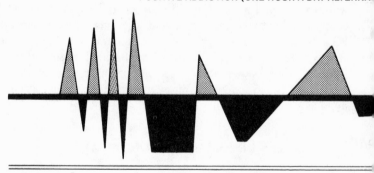

8 STEPS OF RPM (REALITY PERFORMANCE MANAGEMENT)

(1) Make Friends   (2) Ask: What Are   (3) Ask: Is It Helping?   (4) Make a Plan   (5
                        You Doing Now?   to Do Better

OF REALITY THERAPY

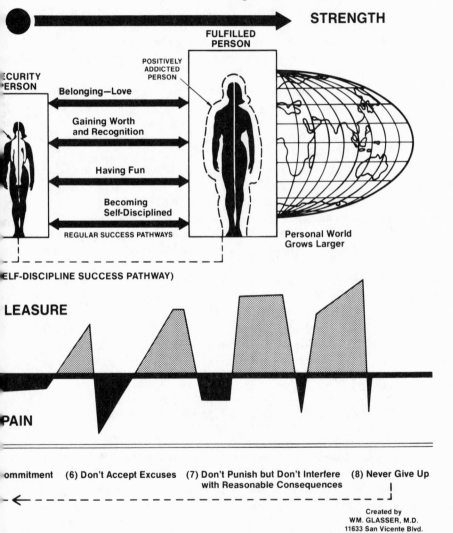

SUCCESS IDENTITY
INVOLVED—Rational, Self—Actualized
Something to Look Forward To

STRENGTH

FULFILLED
PERSON

POSITIVELY
ADDICTED
PERSON

ECURITY
ERSON

Belonging—Love

Gaining Worth
and Recognition

Having Fun

Becoming
Self-Disciplined

REGULAR SUCCESS PATHWAYS

Personal World
Grows Larger

ELF-DISCIPLINE SUCCESS PATHWAY)

LEASURE

PAIN

ommitment   (6) Don't Accept Excuses   (7) Don't Punish but Don't Interfere   (8) Never Give Up
with Reasonable Consequences

Created by
WM. GLASSER, M.D.
11633 San Vicente Blvd.
Los Angeles, CA 90049

This chart may be reproduced.

that in effect says "In most things I am succeeding" or "In most things I am failing." When we say "most things," we mean the goals that we set for ourselves—what we want to do with our lives, based on our background, family and social structure, job, and personality. While there are individual differences in our goals and desires, what most people want from life is remarkably similar. If we generally succeed in getting what we want from life over any reasonable period of time, we come to believe that we are successful, and this belief gradually becomes fixed into an identity: We identify ourselves with success. Likewise, if we are consistently unsuccessful in achieving our goals and desires, we come to believe that we are failures, and this belief, unfortunately, also becomes an identity: We identify ourselves with failure.

Most people believe they are reasonably successful. What concerns us here are those employees who look at themselves and say, "I'm failing." Employees with this negative attitude are not uncommon in any business organization. Some feel they are mild failures, others feel a sense of failure more intensely, and a few extreme cases—alcoholic employees, for example—feel they are almost total failures.

In the Introduction we outlined the eight steps of RPM and showed how they can be used to help failing employees grow stronger. Here we will explain why these employees become the way they are and why they behave the way they do. First, however, we will take a look at the successful employee, because in order to understand failure we must first know what success means and how it can be achieved.

The Successful Employee—The Role of Confidence

Successful people are people who are succeeding at doing the things they want and need to do. Because of that success they have developed a belief in themselves which says, "This is the kind of person I am. I can succeed now, and I will succeed in the future." A glance at the right side of the chart shows that successful people are involved with others in a friendly and satisfactory way, that they tend to live their lives in a rational or sensible manner, and, most important, that they always seem to have something positive to look forward to.

Continuing to look at the right side of the chart, note that the largest black arrow on the right points toward strength. This indicates our conviction that successful people succeed because they have the psychological strength to do what they wish to do. Another way to understand psychological strength is to look at it as confidence. Strong, successful people are confident. If we examine confidence carefully, it is apparent that confidence is a feeling or a belief that people have that they will probably be able to accomplish what they set out to do. Of course, no one can ever be completely sure, but confident people tend to approach most situations with the feeling that the odds are much in their favor. An important reason that the odds are in fact with them is that confidence itself tends to make things work out right. If you are successful, strength or confidence becomes a part of you; it's not turned on and off. There will always be temporary setbacks, failures, and fluctuations. Things may go badly for a while, but confident people don't lose their strength even when they face a reversal. Under certain circumstances, confident people may even welcome a setback. It provides a chance for self-testing, an opportunity to solve the problem at hand and enjoy the satisfying feeling that comes with overcoming obstacles. If everything always went well, confident, competent people would find life dull and uninteresting.

The Failing Employee

In contrast, the people with a failure identity say, "In most things I do not succeed." They feel weak, they lack confidence, and when they set out to do something, they expect to do a poor job. They are not surprised when they fail.

Failing people are illustrated by the three figures on the left side of the chart. Their lives are usually lonely, they tend to be irrational, and since they have little or nothing to look forward to, they live as much as they can in the present. In chapter 2 we will explain in detail how such people struggle with their failure identity and try to make peace with the pain it causes them.

HOW WE FEEL: THE PAYOFF

If we had no emotions we would have little desire to accomplish anything; it is our feelings that motivate us to do what we do with our lives. *How we feel, whether it's good or bad, is the psychological payoff (or price) that we receive or pay for how we behave.*

Keeping in mind the importance of strength, look at the pain-pleasure graph at the bottom of the chart. As you move from the center toward the right, you will note increasing blocks of pleasure and decreasing blocks of pain. While strength and success don't eliminate pain, it is true that as we grow stronger we tend to enjoy life more and more. While it's not possible always to feel good—that is, to lead a 100-percent-successful life—the stronger we are, the better we cope with pain. Therefore, as we move to the right on the chart we see that pleasure increases. At the same time, pain decreases both in amount and in duration as we grow stronger and more competent.

To understand why people behave the way they do, we must understand how they feel. This does not mean, as we will explain in chapter 4, that it is necessary or helpful to talk at length with employees who feel bad about why they feel bad. In order to feel better, we must first begin to behave better; therefore, we advise never talking to employees about how they feel in contexts that are separate from what they do. We do not mean to deny the importance of feelings in our lives. In fact, it is probably true that the only thing that is always real to us is how we feel. We may be fooled about who we are, where we are, what we are doing, and where we are going, but we can never be fooled about how we feel. We feel good or bad, or have mixed feelings, and there is no way to pretend differently.

Feelings give us constant feedback on how we are doing in terms of success and failure. They motivate us to change our behavior when we hurt and to continue behaving as we do when we feel good. This is why we become more conservative as we grow more successful—or even as companies grow more successful. Nobody likes to tamper with success. But the more we fail, the more we hurt. As you move to the left of the chart (until you come to negative addiction), you will see increasing blocks of pain. It is characteristic of failure to be driven by pain, to look for something else to do or someplace else to go. Pain motivates us to change. *The problem is that as we grow more sophisticated and our lives grow more complex, it becomes more difficult to figure out what to do when we hurt.*

THE PATHWAYS TO SUCCESS

For example, if we walk down the street and discover a pebble in our shoe, we know exactly what to do—shake it out. But the pains that most of us experience—depression, tension, anxiety—are nonspecific feelings that do not have clear and immediate causes or solutions. *We have to figure out what has caused us to feel the pain, and the weaker we are, the more difficult this is to do.* This is why Step 4 of RPM—working with the employee to formulate a "get-well" plan—is so important. The inability to plan is a part of the failure identity, and weak people characteristically try to get rid of the pain in any way they can. Most ways they try are not rational and cost them dearly in the long run.

Unlike strong people, who are in control of the present and as a result usually have something positive to look forward to, weak people block out the future. Realizing they are not coping well with their immediate circumstances, they don't heed the consequences of their behavior for the future and are satisfied to do almost anything in a desperate attempt to get rid of the pain of failure, even briefly. Someone who is very weak may turn to alcohol to cushion this misery. The sad truth is that alcohol does temporarily blunt feelings of pain, and a very weak person may feel better when he or she is drunk. In the long run, however, it vastly increases the employee's problems and pushes him or her farther and farther to the left of the chart. Because they are in pain and lose their perspective, weak people are often incapable of making sensible, rational decisions.

Understanding why people who are failing feel the way they do will help you understand why it is so hard to talk to employees who are performing badly and who, obviously, also feel badly. You want the employees to act in a more rational manner, to help themselves do better on the job and thereby feel better, but they don't. Instead, they continue to behave in irrational, emotional, unproductive ways rather than taking hold of themselves and doing something sensible about the pain.

That is why we stress that the best—and only—way to help employees who perform badly, and therefore feel badly, is to relate their feelings to some rational, sensible action that will make them feel better. Good feelings are always the payoffs for good performance.

MODELS OF SUCCESS AND FAILURE

With these general differences between success and failure in mind, let's take a look at the human figures on our chart from the smallest, weakest person on the left to the largest, strongest person on the right. The size of each figure indicates the relative strength. On the left side, from left to right, you will notice Negatively Addicted, Symptom, and Give-Up persons, whom we will discuss in detail in the next chapter. In the center is Security Person, with a small figure inside which we call Survival Person; on the right is a large figure we call Fulfilled Person. Labeled with their major motivations, these five models span the spectrum from those least able to cope to those most able. In this chapter, we will focus first upon Security Person, which includes Survival Person, and then upon the large, strong figure on the success side, Fulfilled Person.

In a sense, the central Security Person stands for us all, because none of us can escape being motivated by security to some degree. For many people, however, security is the main motivator. By this we mean that, under stress, these people immediately concern themselves with simple economic security and little else. When the chips are even partly down, they worry about a roof over their heads, reasonable safety, a job, and perhaps a little money in the bank. Inside Security Person is the small white figure called Survival Person. Few of us come into contact with this person, someone who is struggling each day just to stay alive. Several billion people in the world fall into this category; in Bangladesh and parts of India and South America, the bulk of the population falls into this category. For these unfortunate ones, "success" means a full stomach, warm clothing, and a roof over their heads *tonight*.

In most of our dealings in the world, however, we encounter people who are assured of survival and who are now motivated to keep the security they have achieved. Since all of us have a considerable security motivation, you may think this description fits you. You see yourself engaged in a constant struggle to maintain the job, family, and standard of living you have fought so hard to establish. While we recognize that everyone has days when this may seem to be true, we believe that most if not all the people who read this book have moved their major motivation beyond security.

THE PATHWAYS TO SUCCESS

If, for example, we were guaranteed that we would have adequate food, shelter, and safety but little else, few of us would be willing to accept such a minimally rewarding existence. The basic security of our person alone is not enough. We want more from life, and it is this that most of us struggle for at work and at home. If you look at the chart you will probably see that below Security Person the predominant emotion is pain. While this pain is not as sharp as the pain felt by Symptom Person, it is nonetheless a constant, nagging pain that prevents us from being happy.

Before you disagree with our premise that striving for security to the exclusion of all else is painful, think how you would respond if your boss told you that you were doing a good job and not to worry—"We'll keep you on this particular job until retirement. It won't change much. In fact, it will probably become less important as others rise around you. But don't worry, you will be secure." Would you be satisfied? We don't think so. You would probably say, "I want a job where I have a chance to move ahead, to do something different, to take on different responsibilities, to have some more fun, to travel a little bit, to gain a parking spot—in other words, to receive some recognition beyond just the chance to have a secure, steady job." It's this desire for something more that hurts almost everyone who has little beyond a basic sense of security.

The best way to describe this "something more" is to use a term we often use but rarely think much about—fulfillment. Fulfillment means different things to different people, but as we look at the chart and move to the right from Security Person to Fulfilled Person, there are four arrows or pathways that most of us seem to follow in our efforts to gain fulfillment. These pathways, all of which demand that we have a basic strength, are called here the regular success pathways, because for most of us fulfillment of these pathways is synonymous with success.

In order to succeed we need to gain a sense of belonging, to achieve a feeling of self-worth and receive recognition for a job well done. It is also important that we are able at times to relax and have a little fun. All of these pathways will help us to gain the self-discipline that will continue to move us along in the direction of fulfillment. As we do so, we gain strength and begin to self-actualize. Most of us have the basic strength to get started on this path, and most of us have moved beyond mere security to the stronger, more fulfilled, happier individual labeled Fulfilled Person. We begin the move because it feels good to get rid of the constant, annoying pain associated with merely having security, and we continue the move because the more we progress the better it feels (note the increased blocks of pleasure in the chart). If we didn't have security to begin with, we wouldn't make this move. Therefore, it's obvious that a portion of Security Person (even Survival Person) is within each of us. With security, however, and with a rapidly spinning flywheel, we move as far to the right as we can.

THE FOUR PATHWAYS TO SUCCESS

There are four pathways each person must follow in order to establish a success identity. These are shown on the chart as love and belonging, gaining worth and recognition, having fun, and becoming self-disciplined. Managers attending our seminars frequently ask whether they need to develop all four pathways in their employees. The answer is yes. If any one of these pathways is absent in a person, that person becomes weaker and his or her flywheel slows down, no matter how successful he or she may otherwise be. In the following pages, we will see how each pathway is developed and how you can lead your employees to develop for themselves the pathways they need for success.

The First Pathway: Love and Belonging

The first pathway—love and belonging—means that we need others who care for us and for whom we care ... if we hope to achieve a successful identity. Love, which may mean any one of countless variations, ranging from platonic friendship to deep sexual fulfillment, is not a critical part of the world of work, but belonging is. Belonging or a sense of being among friends is crucial to our well-being and happiness; few of us are willing to settle long for life without it.

Obviously, we can't feel close to every person with whom we come in contact, but we can be warm, friendly, and concerned about those we know and with whom we work. We can make the people around us feel as though we care and, in so doing, we not only will help others to grow stronger but will grow stronger ourselves.

Belonging, or a sense that we are an accepted part of a group—in this case, a working group—spins our identity flywheel in the right direction. Without friendly associations, the flywheel slows down, even if we are financially secure.

The Second Pathway: Gaining Worth and Recognition

As important as money is, once we have established a base of security our sense of fulfillment begins to depend much more upon the feeling that we are doing something worthwhile and being recognized for it. We would wager that a majority of the people reading this book have at some time in their lives left a job that paid well because they were not sufficiently recognized for what they were doing.

A good manager or supervisor takes the time to give employees a chance to say what they are doing that they are proud of. Listen to them; let them go into detail. When you agree, they gain support. And when you disagree, help them work out a way to do the job better. This reinforces their sense of worth; as a result, they feel better, grow stronger, and work harder. The more authority you have, the more you are able to give the recognition that all employees desire and need. (To say, simply, "You did a good job," is good but not enough.)

Whenever we gain recognition from superiors or feel that we are contributing something valuable at work, our flywheel gains momentum. Every manager, from personal experience, knows how good recognition feels and how much it can spur a person to perform. Employees who stagnate on the job and consequently do not receive this kind of positive feedback necessarily search for growth and recognition off the job. They often devote their flywheel strength to outside endeavors that they hope will move them along the pathways to success. While we should, to a certain extent, encourage our people to succeed in endeavors outside the workplace, we must also recognize that if what they do is motivated by their lack of recognition at work, they will gradually lose interest in their job. A good manager should be alert to this and take steps to increase the sense of personal value that employees feel.

People with no avenue for worth and recognition quickly begin to develop a failure identity. They build defenses, such as reducing the quality of their work, to insulate themselves against the pain of insufficient recognition from the boss. As they become less and less productive, they receive less and less recognition; they become problem employees. In chapter 3 we will discuss specific ways in which you can give an employee recognition, the kind of positive reinforcement that will ensure even better performance in the future.

The Third Pathway: Having Fun

Not enough credit is given to the importance of having fun on the job. One philosopher defined fun accurately as "that which you do which you don't have to do." Much of what makes any job worthwhile is a work environment that provides companionship, good feeling, joking, and laughing. No matter how serious the project, more will be accomplished in an enjoyable, nonoppressive atmosphere.

How can you create a pleasant, fun atmosphere at work? A good manager will arrange breaks and lunch periods, and snack and refreshment areas, in such a way as to make them more comfortable and more accessible. You should enjoy having your employees sharing, talking, and laughing during short breaks from work. If they enjoy their moments off, they can accomplish more when they're on. Fun means trying new things, exploring and doing something different, not always because one has to do it or should do it but because sometimes it seems as if it would be fun to do a routine job a new way. A good manager should work with employees in designing some parts of each job with this in mind. With a little ingenuity, some fun can be built into even the most menial tasks.

Employees can also find an element of fun in understanding what is going on, in learning something new, in working on a project that seems important. And there is even a certain joy that comes from comradery and team spirit in working hard to meet an important deadline. There is fun in participating in decision-making and watching that decision become alive at work. Fun can be testing ideas; sometimes the silliest ideas have proved to have the most merit. Fun is Christmas and the World Series and landing on the moon. It's being part of a national experience, landing a big contract, getting a large order out on time. Fun is a co-worker's surprise birthday party. It's chipping in to buy the mailboy something he would never buy on his own, and watching his face when you give it to him. It's taking an inventory on Saturday morning with lots of other people who are relaxed and having a good time. It's shooting the breeze after work, or going fishing together. In these cases fun is intimately tied with work. Work that provides little opportunity for joy puts drag on our flywheel.

A good manager or supervisor knows and remembers that when talking to employees about a problem it helps to be able to get them to crack a smile, to laugh a little, to relax. The old statement "Man does not live by bread alone" applies not only to gaining a sense of self-worth and recognition but also to having fun.

We believe that the no-fun Puritan ethic most of us were raised on is counter-productive, even in the middle of a severe depression or a crisis situation on the job. The people at work who are having fun will almost always outperform the people who take themselves so seriously on the job they can never relax and enjoy themselves. This will be especially evident if a crisis or long-term problem emerges.

The Fourth Pathway: Becoming Self-Disciplined

Self-discipline, planning, and living up to one's commitments lead to a success identity. Self-discipline is different from the other three pathways, but it is included here because we have observed over and over that people who do not have the ability to discipline themselves tend to lead unproductive, miserable lives. Self-discipline and planning go together. Undisciplined people live in a short-term world where tomorrow continually occurs as a surprise rather than as a part of an expected and productive plan.

An effective manager or supervisor looks ahead and tries to develop self-discipline in employees. Help your employees develop self-discipline by letting them do the job themselves. Even if it is easier to do the job yourself, give subordinates a chance to work things out on their own, to solve their own problems. This requires self-discipline on your part, but it pays off when the workload becomes heavy.

Self-discipline is an important pathway to success. Perceived ability to make a plan and follow a disciplined course of action allows a person to feel self-confident.

Self-discipline is also tied to natural consequences. People who are allowed to suffer or enjoy the natural consequences of their decisions are more likely to develop self-discipline than those who are protected from natural consequences. That is why it is critical not to protect people from the results of their actions, unless not to do so would clearly endanger them. The object is to inculcate in employees the desire to negotiate and live up to a responsible plan and commitment, and to do so without excuses. This ability to follow through develops self-discipline and strength.

When we have the strength to move along the four pathways, we then move past Security Person to the stronger, more fulfilled, and happier person shown on the right side of the chart. We call this strong person Fulfilled Person, although he certainly could also be called "rational, fulfilled" because, under stress, the major motivation of this person will be to deal with the problem rationally, sensibly, and logically.

The fulfilled person obviously has many other excellent qualities. This person could also be described as strong, successful, effective, compassionate, loving, creative, imaginative, intuitive, careful, sensitive, disciplined, and fun-loving. In fact, if one reads Abraham Maslow, all twenty-six attributes that make up his "peak" or "self-actualizing" person would be included here, because Fulfilled Person is certainly self-actualizing. In the next chapter we will see that the major difference between Fulfilled Person and the person who is failing is the capacity to be rational rather than emotional under pressure. A fulfilled person has the capacity not only to be strong, self-reliant, and effective but also, when circumstances require, to withstand pain for a long period without behaving irrationally to reduce the pain.

Fulfilled people tend to self-actualize, to use their own initiative rather than waiting for others; they act and lead rather than react or follow. When you have a complex project that requires thought and hard work, these are the people to assign. The more of these people you have working for you, the more, and more pleasantly, will work be done.

Conclusion

The psychological payoff for success is pleasure. The cost of failure is pain. Therefore, all of us, whether at work, in marriage, or in school, strive to move along the four pathways to success. We want to become that larger, more capable, fulfilled person whom we describe as strong, effective, and rational. On the chart to the right of Fulfilled Person is half the globe, indicating that the stronger we are, the larger the world in which we live. This is in contrast to Negatively Addicted Person, the weakest one on the chart, who is trapped far to the left in the tiny world of addiction—drinking, drugs, overeating, or, perhaps, gambling.

Unfortunately, everyone isn't strong. Most problem employees will not yet be on the left side of the chart but they will be moving in that direction. They become lonely and less rational, living their days at work with little or nothing good to look forward to. Their flywheels are slowing down and in some cases have almost stopped.

Why do people—even potentially capable people—settle for a life of failure even though they have so many opportunities for success? In the next chapter, we will look at the people on the failure side of the chart and discover why they act the way they do, both at work and elsewhere. As we gain insight and understanding about their worlds, we can help them function more happily and effectively.

2

The Three Downhill Stages: How Some People Move Toward Failure

Most of us are doing pretty well. We are making a living, doing our jobs, maintaining our family, enjoying our relationships, and having some fun. We know that we aren't perfect, but by and large we see ourselves as effective, reasonably strong, rational people; our flywheels are spinning nicely. But there are among us many who are not so fortunate, many who are failing at work, at school, and in their social relationships. These are the people on the left side of the chart in chapter 1 (reproduced on the following page), and this chapter will help you understand them.

People do not fail all at once. A failure identity occurs in three stages as a person grows weaker and weaker. Moving left in the search for security, the failing person identifies first with the Give-Up (or The-Heck-With-It) Person, then with the Symptom Person, and finally, almost totally depleted in strength, with the Negatively Addicted Person. Each move is a desperate, *irrational* attempt to reduce the pain associated with failure, but each move unfortunately makes things worse, not better. The person's flywheel slows down more and more.

Failure occurs for many reasons. At some time in their lives, some people find themselves lacking the strength to move toward success; they suffer from a lack of love or sense of self-worth, and their lives become joyless. Unable to move to the right, and hurting because they seem locked into a pattern of painful unfulfillment, they become more and more desperate in their efforts to get rid of the pain. This desperation leads to irrationality, to the unfortunate choices that these people begin to make in their lives.

THE BASIC CONCEPTS OF REALITY THERAPY

FAILURE IDENTITY
LONELY—Less Rational

Little or Nothing to Look Forward To

WEAKNESS ⟵

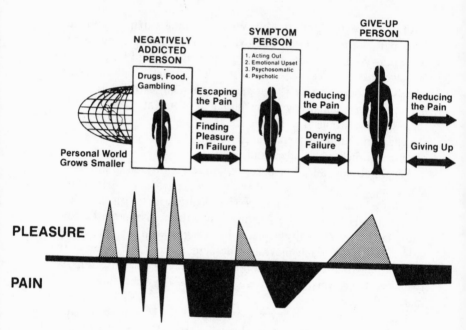

NEGATIVELY ADDICTED PERSON

Drugs, Food, Gambling

Personal World Grows Smaller

Escaping the Pain

Finding Pleasure in Failure

SYMPTOM PERSON

1. Acting Out
2. Emotional Upset
3. Psychosomatic
4. Psychotic

Reducing the Pain

Denying Failure

GIVE-UP PERSON

Reducing the Pain

Giving Up

PLEASURE

PAIN

Created by
WM. GLASSER, M.D.
11633 San Vicente Blvd.
Los Angeles, CA 90049

This chart may be reproduced.

THE FIRST STAGE OF FAILURE: THE GIVE-UP PERSON

There are many reasons that people lack strength. They may have come from a broken family, had too much criticism as a child, failed in school, been rejected in love or friendship, or suffered from bad health. Maybe they did well as children, and in the insulated world of school, but can't make the adjustment as adults out in the harsh real world. No matter what the reason for lack of strength and bad performance, if they can't gather the strength to begin to succeed on the job, they will begin to think of themselves as failures. Then they will choose to move their lives to the failure side of the chart.

Suppose you have an employee whose work is always marginal and who usually gets assignments in late. You try giving extra support and attention, but it doesn't provide any motivation. You call the employee into your office to discuss an assignment that the worker has submitted late and that requires a considerable amount of revision. After a few friendly words, you have hardly started when the employee blurts out, "It's the best I can do. There are only eight hours in a day. Besides, it's good enough for the finance department anyway. They change everything when they make out their final reports, so why should I break my back?"

Here you are dealing with someone in the first stages of failure, a person shown on the chart as a Give-Up Person. Such employees may have a million excuses, but the fact is that they really aren't putting much effort into the job. They've given up and have accepted themselves as mediocre performers at best. They have joined a large group of people who not only give up on their jobs, but also may give up on their education, their wives, their families, and even, in some cases, on the fun of recreational activities, such as golf or tennis or fishing. They give up because they honestly believe that even if they make the effort they still won't succeed.

Not long ago employees just didn't tell a boss that they couldn't do a job. Unless the employee was related to the owner of the business, such a statement would lead to immediate firing. Even today, it's extremely unusual to have an employee actually say "I give up, I can't do it" or "The heck with it, it's good enough." What employees do instead is give up in a series of subtle ways, so that it seems as if they are working, but they really are doing little or nothing on the job, or performing far below their capabilities.

As a manager or supervisor, you should be constantly on the lookout for the following signs of giving up.

- The employee avoids taking on any extra responsibility at all. He or she has an "it's not worth the money to do all that" attitude. This often occurs after an employee expected a promotion or raise and was turned down.
- The employee lacks initiative. He or she gives up by forcing the supervisor to explain exactly what has to be done next. No matter how small the problem, the boss is forced to solve it. There is no attempt to hustle or take command of the work situation.
- The employee refuses to make decisions, even when the decision involves the employee directly. He or she simply says, "I don't know. That's up to you."
- The employee procrastinates by either waiting too long to tackle the assignment or spreading the work out over an unreasonable length of time. Sometimes, the worker even misplaces the assignment, perhaps subconsciously hoping it will go away.
- The employee is loaded with excuses that are repeated like a broken record. He or she appears less and less on the job, using up sick leave, arriving late, taking long lunches, leaving early. It appears that the worker no longer cares about the job.
- The employee's work becomes shoddy and barely passable—engineers hand in sloppy specifications, secretaries type letters poorly, for example. The employee makes little or no effort to improve no matter how hard he or she is prodded.
- The employee tries to hide a poor performance behind procedures. He or she becomes more interested in form than substance. The person defines the job in such a way as to easily defend himself or herself, if things go wrong, and at the same time blame everything on others who are not following the correct procedures.

There isn't a supervisor who hasn't run into Give-Up Person at some time or other. In fact, many of you may have one or more such persons working for you right now. Think about them, and try to discover how they are telling you they have given up.

The Pleasure of Giving Up

Why do people give up on the job? Why do they produce less or hand in work that is poorly done or hide behind excuses? A quick glance at the chart in chapter 1 will show you the major reason why people give up: It feels good. Note on the Pleasure-Pain graph (at the bottom of the chart) the temporary burst of pleasure that comes when people begin to live by the mottoes "The heck with it," "It's not important," "I don't care." The real reason underlying their decision to give up is that they honestly don't believe they have the strength to succeed. Giving up makes sense to them because, convinced they are bound to fail, it seems less painful just to let go altogether rather than try and fail and risk even greater pain.

All of us recognize the temporary relief we feel when we say "The heck with it." For example, we have guests to our house, everyone has a good time, but at the end of the evening the house and the kitchen are a mess. Relaxed but tired, we look at the mess and say, "The heck with it." It feels so good just to ignore the mess and go to bed, hoping that the good dish fairy will get up in the middle of the night and make everything spic and span by morning. In the morning we have to face the reality that we have to do the cleaning up ourselves, but at least we had the pleasure of a temporary reprieve from an unpleasant task.

Give-up people live their lives for the small amount of relief they get every time they give up. They just quit "washing the dishes," and for a while the relief they feel becomes the major pleasure in their lives.

We do not wish to imply that people give up easily or quickly. They don't. Most people, even weak people, try hard. Even the employee now sitting in your office whom you are desperately trying to motivate may have put in a lot of effort before finally caving in. What you see before you is the result of a lot of anguish. But, lacking strength, the employee finally made the irrational decision to give up rather than to keep trying.

As you can see by the chart, giving up relieves the pain only temporarily. But keep in mind that failing people have a very limited sense of the future. If they think of the future at all, they think of it as something ominous, and they try to live in the present. Therefore, to tell these employees that everything will catch up with them in the future rarely makes an impression. They don't hear you. All they are aware of is the internal voice that keeps repeating, "I am not going to make it. There is no sense in trying. It hurts too much. Why hassle with the situation any longer?" Even the thought of losing their jobs may become attractive. No job, no pain. And if this thought bothers them, they persuade themselves that they just can't do it, that they might as well quit.

The Trouble with Giving Up

The trouble with giving up is obvious. The malaise spreads, like rust. It starts slowly and insidiously, but if you don't treat it, it will only get worse and worse. We finish an assignment knowing that it's not quite up to par and rationalize to ourselves that "it's good enough." It gets by, we enjoy getting away with it, and we try it again. As we fall into this trap, however, our flywheel spins more slowly. Inside, we are well aware that we are putting less and less spin on our wheel. More and more we say, "The heck with it," and the give-up approach spreads to other areas of our lives. Before long, we are trapped into chronically making the decision to give up.

People with the give-up mentality that are perhaps the most distressing are young people who give up in school. First they stop trying, then they make trouble. They may end up taking drugs and drinking heavily. But whatever they do later, giving up is their first step. Unless someone can persuade them to start trying, persuade them that school—either academic or vocational—is important, their ability to live as effective, productive, happy people may end as early as junior high.

Many companies employ these school failures. When they begin to fail on the job they almost always say, "I don't care what happens to me" or "Fire me, so what? I'll collect unemployment." If such employees hang on for a while and then become protected by union contracts, civil service regulations, or other company constraints that make it difficult to terminate them, they become a serious psychological burden to the productive people in the company who have to associate with them, even if they do not constitute a pressing economic burden. That's why we believe it is so important for you to start applying the RPM approach in your company as soon as possible. If you understand why these people act the way they do, and if you work with them to develop a better plan and to help them become stronger, they too can become effective workers.

As you can see from the Pleasure-Pain graph at the bottom of the chart, the decision to give up relieves the immediate pain and provides a temporary feeling of pleasure. But giving up works only for a while; the pleasure soon diminishes, the pain and frustration return. Only now it's worse than before, because the person has experienced even more failure.

At this point the person faces another choice. Spurred on by this new pain, many people see the benefits of a productive life and begin to move to the right. They realize that giving up didn't work. They gather themselves together, tap what residual strength they have left in their flywheel, and start moving again. Many others, however, make a more negative choice. They choose to move another step to the left, to go from Give-Up Person to Symptom Person, the next stage in the downhill drift toward failure.

THE SECOND STAGE OF FAILURE: THE SYMPTOM PERSON

Driven by renewed pain and diminished strength, Give-Up Person makes a further desperate choice, choosing to develop one or more psychological symptoms. Note on the chart at the beginning of this chapter that under Symptom Person four major symptoms are listed: (1) Acting Out; (2) Emotional Upset (tension, anxiety, depression); (3) Psychosomatic (sickness, real or imagined, connected to above symptoms); (4) Psychotic (irrationality, ultimately leading to psychosis).

Acting Out

In choosing the first symptom, Acting Out, people who previously said "The heck with it" about their work now say "The heck with it" with regard to the way society or the boss or the company says to run things. Acting Out people say, "I'll do it my way. What do they know? I've got a better way, and if they don't like it, they can lump it." They begin more and more to live by their own rules and to disregard the rules of the world around them. In a business organization, acting out might exhibit itself in unauthorized absences, coming to work late, starting trouble, arguing, fighting, refusing to answer the phone, or misusing or stealing company property.

By the time people have reached the stage of choosing the Acting Out symptom, they are suffering so much and are so concerned with their own feelings that they care little about the feelings of others. If others get upset because of their behavior, they say, "That's their problem, not mine." Acting out starts with tantrums in childhood, continues for many in school in the refusal to follow school rules, and often ends in delinquency or with the student being sent to reform school. But regardless of the consequences, Acting Out people live almost entirely for the present, doing what they do because it feels good at the time. Suddenly, as they feel free to do their own thing, the pain and frustration are gone.

If such employees had the psychological strength and self-understanding to appreciate the consequences of how they behave, they wouldn't act out. They are unable to get the perspective they need to curb their behavior, and they need a manager's help. The only solution to the problem of acting out is to stop such people from breaking the rules and, when they are stopped, to help them to gain the strength and confidence to do things in a better way. Remem-

SYMPTOMS OF ACTING OUT

- Fighting with others
- Disregarding rules and procedures
- Misplacing important papers
- Resisting authority
- Being absent at critical times
- Breaking or damaging equipment
- Waiting to be told what to do and following directions explicitly, without thinking
- Griping excessively and maliciously
- Hurting other people physically or with words
- Disregarding reality and good advice

ber, if people who act out are permitted to continue their self-destructive behavior, they cannot be helped.

We all give up once in a while. Many of us break a rule occasionally, but we don't think of ourselves as giving up or acting out. Therefore, it is important to realize that none of us exists 100 percent in any single position on the chart. We exist *predominantly* in one place, but even the strongest, most rational, and most fulfilled person continues to be concerned with security, still gives up once in a while, still occasionally displays a negative symptom, and perhaps even gets drunk every so often when the world seems too difficult. But we must understand that even with these upsets and lapses in behavior, most of us are strong enough to live predominantly to the right of Security Person. We correct our mistakes or live with them, but we don't feel or act like failures.

No one is 100 percent strong or 100 percent weak. Human beings are more complex than that. Most of us have the inner strength to help ourselves when we recognize we are making choices that lead to failure. Even employees who have apparently given up or have chosen to develop negative symptoms have elements of strength inside that can be tapped to help them get back on the pathway to success.

The kinds of people who choose to act out by hurting others or by flagrantly violating rules are usually not kept on any job for any length of time. But when the acting out is subtle, they often get away with it for a long time before what they are doing becomes obvious. For these people, Step 2 of RPM is very important. You must discuss with them precisely what they are doing and then, with their cooperation, develop a plan to stop it. If you do not do this as soon as the behavior pattern emerges, it will be increasingly difficult to get them to change. You will become more and more annoyed at how cleverly they talk all around their behavior and avoid facing what they are doing. You must take a firm stand immediately or they will continue to manipulate you in a thousand subtle and destructive ways.

Emotional Upset

Equally as common as employees who act out are employees who exhibit the second type of symptom, emotional upset, most often

---

SYMPTOMS OF DEPRESSION

- Uninvolvement and no sense of belonging
- Anxiousness
- Sadness
- Shuffling from place to place
- Spiritlessness
- Humorlessness
- Staring vacantly
- Withdrawing and becoming isolated and detached
- Fatigue
- Work output slowing down considerably
- Avoidance of taking on anything new or extra
- Being sick, late, and absent excessively
- Crying

---

seen as tension, anxiety, and depression. If, for example, you have an employee who is seriously depressed, you can expect that person to do little or no work, because the depression robs him or her of the energy needed to be productive.

We do not often run into severely depressed people at work because those with severe psychological problems generally stay at home. However, we do have employees whose emotional upsets show up in less obvious ways. They refuse to become involved with the people around them, and they get out of touch with the work itself. They do their work in a spiritless fashion and lose their sense of humor. They act and look tired most of the time. Sometimes, for insignificant reasons, they fly off the handle and then quickly lapse back into sadness and depression. While they continue to function, they are able to keep up with only the most routine jobs.

People seem to *choose* to be depressed when giving up no longer works. Why? Because—as miserable as depression is—*no one, including themselves, expects a depressed person to do very much. They may suffer but they are off the hook.* It's hard to understand why anyone would choose to be depressed. The reason is that depressed people aren't able to use their good sense. Lacking strength, they lose their ability to behave rationally. When they recover their strength and are again capable of thinking clearly, they stop choosing depression.

Painful as it is, depression allows failing people to deny responsibility for their failure. When you try to get depressed people going, they blame their inability to do anything on their misery. And you feel like Simon Legree when you try to push them. By enlisting your sympathy—which isn't hard if they are obviously miserable—they turn the tables and make you feel cruel when you point out that work is piling up. You become trapped into listening more and more to their emotional problems, and the more you appear to sympathize, the easier it is for them to deny their part in the failure. As they continue to fail, it becomes more difficult, if not impossible, for them to recognize that they are *choosing* to be depressed in order to avoid facing their inadequacies.

If you are supervising a depressed person, it is understandable that you tend to expect less and less. It's upsetting even to be with that person. So you tend to avoid him or her and don't push. In these ways you feed the depression. This is why we advise strongly that you listen to only a minimum of their upset and say as soon as possible "OK, you're depressed, you're upset. But look. What are you doing? Couldn't we figure out how you might get started back to work? Because if you do, I'm sure you'll feel better."

Psychosomatic Illness

The third set of symptoms, becoming physically sick, is perhaps the symptom most commonly found in people who work under pressure. Such people may perform well, sometimes very well, even when they are overloaded with work (working twelve hours a day for weeks on end), but eventually the pressure gets to them and they become sick. In many cases, people with psychosomatic or stress illness are capable, hardworking people who for the most part are temporarily overloaded. Their sickness may be their way of saying "I can't do it any longer." These people are too strong and too much in control of themselves to give up or to choose another symptom. But when they become sick, they are in a sense trying to justify their feeling that they need some relief. It is frightening how under conditions of extreme stress some people can move so quickly from being rational and effective to being sick. Good managers who

---

SYMPTOMS OF PSYCHOSOMATIC SICKNESS

- Aches and pains
- Headaches
- Back troubles
- Neck aches
- Chronic fatigue
- Problems with teeth and gums
- Insomnia
- Chronic medical troubles of a non-specific nature
- Chronic laryngitis
- Shortness of breath
- Some forms of heart trouble, ulcers, allergies, and ar-thritis may be partly psychosomatic in origin

---

see a competent employee start to become sick should try to lighten the load on that person. If the employee gets a respite, he or she may snap back and begin to function well again. If the load isn't lightened, however, the sickness may progress to the point where the employee will need to take time off to recuperate.

Psychosomatic symptoms include aches and pains, headaches, backaches, neck aches, feeling fatigued or not up to par, and insomnia. The symptoms are rarely accompanied by emotional disturbance. In other words, the person feels fine emotionally; he or she gets upset physically instead of emotionally. If an employee suffers from any of these symptoms or from a more severe psychosomatic illness, he or she will be forced to see a doctor, and the situation will generally be out of the hands of the manager. A good manager, however, may recognize that a person needs medical care and will not only suggest it but will try to make the time available for the employee to do so, even if it means leaving work to go see the doctor.

Psychosomatic sickness is much more complex than described here. But we want to emphasize that, for the most part, people at work who choose psychosomatic symptoms are generally capable, functional people who are temporarily overloaded. They are valuable employees, and when they are helped to overcome their temporary setback, they will be grateful and even more valuable in the future.

Psychosis

Once in a while you may encounter someone on the job who is psychotic. Here, you have an example of people who have chosen the fourth symptom, leaving the real world and moving into a world in their own heads. These people are obviously out of touch with reality. In leaving reality, they may latch on to any kind of thinking or behavior that makes sense to them *but only to them.* If and when you run across someone like this either at work or in your personal life, urge him or her to seek professional help. Treat such people calmly and with understanding, but try to get them to take a sick leave and insist that their family or friends—or someone—take them to see a qualified mental health counselor. Psychotic people can be very frightening to a lay person, and it's much better to refer them to a professional, who can give them proper treatment, than to try to work with them on the job.

Regardless of the symptom a person chooses, it is clear that the act of choosing a symptom is an irrational attempt to get relief from feelings of pain and failure. Since the symptom doesn't in any way solve the problem, the person ends up weaker and in more pain than before he or she made the choice. And the cycle repeats itself—the person clings to the symptom all the more tightly because, even though it doesn't help, it's all that seems to be left.

Caught in this circular trap, many people do seek help. It's obvious to them that they are in a miserable and painful position and that they need help to get their flywheels spinning again. It's not uncommon for people locked into a painful symptom to seek professional counseling, and a good manager or supervisor should encourage employees to do so. Professional counseling, supplemented by an understanding manager, can in many cases lead even a symptomatic person to pull together and get the flywheel going once more.

THE THIRD STAGE OF FAILURE: THE NEGATIVELY ADDICTED PERSON

When locked into the pain and misery of a symptom, most people try to do something constructive about it. Unfortunately, there are a large number of people, including many who have responsible, high-paying jobs, who choose to try to escape completely from the pain, to find a way to feel good even though they are seriously failing. Such people choose addiction, and alcohol is by far the most common addictive substance to which they turn. Unlike giving up or choosing a symptom—both of which ultimately produce even more pain—*addiction not only relieves the pain but allows the person to find pleasure in failure.*

We distinguish between two types of addiction: positive addiction and negative addiction. A positive addiction is a beneficial habit or activity, such as running, meditating, swimming, or yoga, which makes us feel better and grow stronger and to which we gradually become addicted. Like people who are negatively addicted, people who are positively addicted find they must keep up the addiction or suffer the pain and misery of withdrawal (think, for example, of the discomfort felt by a jogger who returns to the track after an extended absence). Unlike negative addictions, however, positive addictions are pathways to strength; they make us stronger, not weaker, and they put a lot of spin in our wheels.

Negative addictions, on the other hand, are a last resort for a person who feels he or she is failing. They are an irrational attempt to escape from a painful reality, and, once established, they are extremely difficult to shake. As a manager or supervisor, the negative addiction with which you will most likely be concerned is alcoholism.

In the beginning, alcoholism is difficult to recognize. The signs are subtle: reduced performance, sloppiness, absenteeism, increased requests for a great deal of sick leave, accompanied by a wide variety of vague complaints. Between these signs of slipping performance are episodes of good performance; the person becomes his or her old self again. But just as you become relaxed, relieved that things are again going well, the employee slips back into a pattern of vague complaints, inefficient performance, and absenteeism. The periods of competence become shorter and the periods of ineffectiveness increase as the employee continues to drink, letting the alcohol take over more and more. (The more quickly a manager or supervisor who suspects an employee is an alcoholic acts, the better the chance that the person can be helped. We will discuss in detail in chapter 10 what you should do when confronted with an alcoholic employee.)

Alcohol and other drugs are addictive because, besides eliminating pain, they consistently provide pleasure. Addictive drugs break the basic survival chain that couples pain with poor performance. The purpose of pain is to warn us that what we are doing is dangerous, but when we become involved with an addictive drug this warning system is inactivated. In such a case, we can continue performing poorly, often to the point where our lives are in danger. And as we indulge regularly in the addictive drug, we lose sight of the harm we are causing ourselves.

Once an employee becomes negatively addicted, his or her flywheel stops completely and then reverses. It begins to spin backward, and as it spins it provides strength and momentum only for further addiction, to procure more alcohol and to rationalize more drinking. This is why the world of the Negatively Addicted Person is so small, as depicted on the far left side of our chart.

Because alcoholics are weak, because their whole life is consumed with the pleasure that drinking provides, they fail to grasp that everything they previously held important is now slipping away. Once addicted, alcoholics not only continue when sober to suffer the pain of the symptom that led them to addiction, but beyond that, they experience the severe withdrawal pain that accompanies any attempt to give up alcohol. More and more, they drink not because their life is unproductive or to relieve symptoms but because if they stop drinking they acutely miss the chemical. To avoid this pain of withdrawal, they drink more and still more. While drinkers have different drinking patterns in the beginning (some drink every day, some only in the evenings or on weekends), these patterns tend to be unstable, and in each instance more and more drinking occurs.

Six percent of all adults are alcoholics, and many more are problem drinkers verging toward alcoholism. If left alone, most of these people will soon find themselves unable to perform productively. It is a good manager's responsibility to try to do something to help when an employee has this problem.

We have now defined the RPM approach, stated its objectives, and described in detail how different kinds of employees can benefit from its methods. In the next chapters, we will explain the eight steps of RPM and show how you can best put RPM to work for you.

3

RPM Step 1: Establish a Good Working Relationship with Employees, Especially the Ones Who Are Doing Poorly

What you as a manager or supervisor want are employees who will do a responsible job, avoid problems, and, if problems do arise, use their own initiative and good sense to solve them. In other words, you want employees who are moving toward success, strength, and self-discipline. When their flywheels spin with strength, yours does also. Each step of RPM is designed to help build your employees' confidence and effectiveness, thereby moving them toward the success and growth side of the chart. We begin with Step 1, where we consider how to establish a good working relationship with your employees and how to maintain it even when things go wrong.

Remember, when employees are slipping they may go down through each failure stage but when they start to gain strength they may move quickly and directly to the success side without moving up through the failure stages. Keep these stages on the chart in mind, but remember the crucial point is the direction in which an employee is moving. RPM will get the flywheel going and start the employee moving to the right.

Let's face it. As easy as it is to form a warm relationship with good employees, it is that much harder to communicate in the same friendly fashion with those who are performing badly. Their performance aggravates and upsets you and makes you doubt your own effectiveness as a manager or supervisor. As the situation becomes more apparent, your natural inclination is to see as little of such employees as possible. Yet we maintain that if you are going to help them improve their performance, your best chance is to try to establish friendly contact. Unless you do so, it will be difficult if not impossible to break their bad behavior pattern and rechannel their energy toward a more productive performance in the future.

Building a good working relationship is like putting money in the bank. When you build a reserve on a daily basis, there will be good-will to draw against when problems arise. Employees who feel that the only reason you call them into your office is to kick them around are certain to become defensive. The ideas we are about to propose may at first seem oversimplified, but they are not. As you read them, think about problem employees you have had to deal with, and ask yourself whether you are following the strength-building strategies we suggest.

Assume for a moment that you are once again having problems with Bob, our chronically troublesome Acme accounts receivable man. He has just delivered a report indicating that several big-dollar customers have not paid Acme for ninety days. You, his manager, are really disturbed by this unpleasant surprise. But don't call Bob into your office until you cool down. Call him in when you have time, when you are feeling reasonably comfortable with yourself, and when you are not in the middle of another problem in which he is involved. When Bob comes to your office, don't answer the phone, write a letter, look out the window, or refer to your watch. Employees like Bob cost you valuable time, and to help them do better you must give them your undivided attention, even if just for a short period. Make Bob feel comfortable, shake hands, offer coffee, and if your office is roomy come out from behind your desk, and sit beside him. Ask something about his life away from work, for example, about his family, his wife, their children, his interests or hobbies. Spend several minutes letting him know you have some warm, friendly concern for him both as an employee and as a person outside of work. Bob will know that he is being called into your office because he is not performing well. And he will also sense that this friendly approach is probably a prelude to getting down to the business of his poor performance. But the fact that he understands what you're doing will not in any way diminish the effectiveness of this approach. Even if you feel a little bit uneasy at the beginning, that feeling will disappear as you proceed through the steps of RPM. And this first part of the first step—getting to talk to one another—is vital.

After a few minutes of general discussion, when Bob feels relatively comfortable, your next step is to proceed to the business at hand: Bob's performance. If you move too abruptly to the problem, Bob will become too defensive to maintain the necessary rapport. It is best to start on a positive note by discussing some part of his performance that is satisfactory. Everyone has an area of competence, so spend a little time recognizing what he is doing well. We recognize that this is hard to do, especially when you are aggravated by an employee's poor performance. It will require of you a different kind of firmness, one that is much more difficult to achieve than the instinctive nonaccepting, critical attitude you may have used in the past. If you follow this advice, however, Bob will feel a greater sense of acceptance. He will feel that you want to help him rather than tear him down. The stage will be better set to get the facts on the table and improve his subsequent performance.

We emphasize that this approach should be used whether the problem is of short or long duration and whether it is simple or complex. You should be warm and supportive if you want the employee to do better.

STRATEGIES FOR ESTABLISHING A GOOD RELATIONSHIP

Here are thirteen strategies a manager or supervisor can use to put good relations in the bank for a rainy day.

1. Learn how to give recognition for things that are going right. We all know from personal experience how important this is. In the next section we discuss when to give an employee recognition, the best way to do this, and when not to give recognition.
2. Take your time when talking to an employee. Learn to say "We have time" when you have a meeting concerning an employee's performance. When someone in authority says there is time, the meeting generally takes less time.
3. Avoid dealing with the employee at the height of a crisis or problem. Both of you will be at your worst.
4. Never ask a question if you are not prepared to listen to the answer. If you ask a proud father how his kids are doing in Little League, don't change the subject in the middle of his reply.

5. Convey your respect for the employee by keeping your appointments and being on time. This is especially important for employees who have a problem with punctuality. Setting an example is a powerful way to teach. If your employee is the kind of person who tends to take up too much of your time with irrelevant matters, reverse the normal procedure and talk business first. When that is accomplished, discuss personal matters for the time you have left.

6. Never criticize or berate anyone in front of others. This not only slows down an employee's flywheel but shatters it as well.

7. Give the employee quality time. The amount of time you give a person is less important than giving your uninterrupted, undivided attention.

8. Make work fun whenever you can. Easy banter, birthday celebrations, and nice surprises add reserve spin to our flywheels.

9. Be reliable and consistent with your employees. It is easy for managers to show they care when things go well. It is more difficult—but more important—to show warmth when things go badly. The employee who feels the boss has a steadfast concern for his or her welfare will reciprocate in kind.

10. Don't overreact when things go wrong. Goodwill is hard to build up and easy to knock down. The manager who overreacts when something goes wrong can destroy a year of rapport in a few minutes. Develop some cooling off tactics of your own, like counting to one hundred when you're angry. When you get extremely upset, do as Abe Lincoln did: write a long letter to the person who is frustrating you and then tear it up.

11. Don't knock an employee when he or she fails when trying something new. Many managers give a great deal of lip service to encouraging their employees to be more assertive and innovative. But when things go wrong, they berate the employee for doing the very things they were encouraged to do.

12. Try to avoid criticism. Criticizing is a skill that even the most tactful managers find difficult to master. In the next chapters we will show many specific ways to deal with people and get them to improve their performance without directly criticizing.

13. Don't let a credibility gap develop between you and your subordinates. Be honest with them. Whether the news you bring is good or bad, they will think more of you for it.

THE BEST WAY TO GIVE RECOGNITION
FOR GOOD WORK

There is an old Japanese saying that one of the greatest pleasures in life is having someone in authority praise you in front of others. It is not always possible or prudent for a manager or supervisor to do this, but a little pat on the back in front of others puts a lot of spin in people's flywheels. A good manager learns to do this in a way that does not put others down. But whether others are present or not, good work should always be praised.

The key to giving recognition is understanding that when people do a good job they want the boss to recognize *in detail* how it was done. The manager who merely says "You did a good job" is providing the employee with some satisfaction, but not nearly as much as just a little more effort could produce. When giving recognition, *be specific and go into detail.* Let the employee explain how he or she specifically achieved a difficult or unusual success on the job. Then commend the employee in a step-by-step fashion as the achievement is described. For example, when your son polishes the car, you don't just tell him what a good job he did, you mention that the chrome is especially nice around the lights and the grill, and you ask him how he got it to shine so nicely. The same principle applies in dealing with an employee. A worker will be pleased to tell you specifically how the feat was accomplished and will try hard to achieve similar recognition another time.

One of the most difficult problems you will run into as a manager or supervisor is giving recognition to an employee whose performance is below par but who has recently made some progress. To do so, the manager should compliment the person on the achievement and follow the principle of specific recognition as much as possible. But the manager should be honest and state that while there has indeed been improvement, the overall performance remains below standard. Before the employee reacts to what now may seem to be a left-handed compliment, the manager should right then and there negotiate a new and more responsible plan to which the employee can become committed (see RPM Steps 4 and 5). By doing this, you show the employee that you have overall confidence in him or her, and the employee can face the still inadequate performance with renewed strength. Remember, you can never build individuals up by tearing them down!

Never praise an employee who has not earned it. If you do so, you weaken both that person and your relationship, because the employee will know that the recognition is phony, not real. The person who has not earned praise should be treated honestly, but also warmly and compassionately. Such treatment can convey the message that improvement will bring praise. The manager can also honestly say, "I would like to give you some recognition, but you just haven't reached the point where I can. Let's take a good look at where you have to go. When you get there, I want to be the first to pat you on the back."

Conclusion

If any of you feel hesitant or uncomfortable about putting Step 1 of RPM to work, especially with an employee who you believe is incompetent, keep in mind that we do not ask you to accept incompetence. All we are saying is that poor performance is best corrected from a base of acceptance rather than rejection. Do not mistake acceptance for softness, passivity, or wishy-washiness. It is none of these. In fact, you will find that acceptance requires of you more strength and firmness than rejection or anger ever could.

If Step 1 or any of the following steps of RPM were easy, managers would be using them. But they're not easy. Building and maintaining friendly rapport with an incompetent or erratic employee is hard for both manager and employee. Both of you must work at it, not only when things go wrong but on a day-to-day basis. It is difficult for managers because it is easier to reject employees who perform badly than to accept them. Likewise, it is difficult for employees, because once they believe that the manager accepts and supports them, they can no longer excuse their lack of performance on the basis that the boss doesn't know what they're doing or doesn't like them. The manager's acceptance helps employees to feel a sense of belonging and, with that, the strength to focus on the problem; that is, on their own performance and what can be done about it.

4

RPM Steps 2 and 3: Get the Facts on the Table and Get the Employee's Evaluation

In RPM Step 1 you called Bob, the Acme Cabinet Company accounts receivable clerk, in for a conference. You were warm, accepting, and noncritical, but as you attempted to get the facts on the table, there was disagreement. Before you knew it, there were unpleasant feelings about what the facts actually were and who was to blame. If this happens to you, as it does to so many managers, then the conference will have little value, and future dealings with the same employee will be difficult.

How can you put the facts on the table without creating hard feelings? Keep in mind these three easy-to-remember rules:

Rule 1: Avoid dwelling on past problems. Stick to what is going on right now, even if the employee has made the same mistake twenty times before. Simply stated, don't *you* bring up the past. If the employee brings up the past to justify certain actions, shift the discussion back to the present.

Rule 2: Don't get bogged down with discussion about how anyone may feel about the problem. Move to discuss performance as quickly as possible. Discourage any talk about feelings or frustrations unless the feelings are directly related to present performance.

Rule 3: Do all you can to let the employee evaluate his or her present performance, including what he or she is doing to help the situation and/or to make matters worse.

These rules look simple, but they're not. They require a conscious effort on your part and a commitment to avoid falling into habitual patterns of behavior. Think about it. How many times have you said to an employee, "That's the third time I've told you about keeping the record straight. When are you going to learn?" It is so easy to fall into a pattern like this. You feel righteous when saying it, because it's so true. But all it does is guarantee that things will not get better. If you harp on past mistakes, your meeting will be a waste of time. Let's see how these rules can be applied to another problem employee at the Acme Cabinet Company.

John is a knowledgeable but careless design man in Acme's custom kitchen cabinet department. His job is to translate the requirements of building contractors and their clients into a set of workable plans that not only satisfy their aesthetic needs but also can be produced and installed at minimum cost. John does most things well. He is creative, good with customers, and knowledgeable about production. His major flaw is that he doesn't pay enough attention to details.

John's problem is driving his boss crazy. A simple mistake, like not checking the precise dimensions of a stove or refrigerator, costs the company a great deal of time and money because it means that a set of cabinets for as many as one hundred new houses must be redone. The delay usually results in a very angry customer. The manager is aware of John's best and worst traits and has spoken with him often about them. John always promises to be more careful, but he continues to make careless mistakes. However, it would be unwise to terminate John, because it takes so long to train people in the intricacies of the custom cabinet business, and he is generally a competent man.

Well, here we are again. John has just made another $10,000 mistake, and a good customer is furious. John assumed, without checking, that the built-in oven was a standard 27 inches wide, and he designed all the kitchen cabinets around it. But the customer had specified a 30-inch oven, a fact that was discovered by the installers after all the cabinets had been made. Now they must be changed. Acme is in an uproar. The vice-president has just called John's boss on the carpet for the goof-up. Now the boss wants to get to John. Is there any way the manager can help John be more careful?

First, following Step 1 of RPM, the manager should not talk to him at the moment of crisis, because John will be too defensive. Wait until tomorrow to discuss his chronic carelessness, then if he's had a good day, ask him to come to the office. Chronic, recurring problems can wait a day; get to them on the first good day.

With an employee such as John, who has worked with the manager for a long time, a few words to make him comfortable are all that are needed before talking about his current mistake. If it were harder to establish a friendly rapport with him, the manager would need to spend more time laying the groundwork. Remember from Step 1, you can't effectively get to the core of any problem until both of you feel comfortable, unhurried, and friendly.

RPM STEP 2: GET THE FACTS ON THE TABLE

Avoid Talking About Past Mistakes

Keeping Rule 1 in mind, don't start from the past. The past is full of old events and excuses, and neither of you will ever agree on what happened then. With John, the place to start is yesterday's problem. You are on firm ground because you know he can do good work and what you are trying to do is set the stage to develop a plan (RPM Step 4) to help him become more careful in the future. Start by asking a simple, friendly question. Use your own words, but say something like this: "Why do you think I called you in today?" Since he knows there was a problem with the cabinets, he very well might say, "Well, I thought you might be concerned about the mistake I made yesterday." He may then try to gloss over the seriousness of the situation, covering a lot of other ground in his effort to justify his "occasional" lapses. Tactfully but firmly, and with no reference to his understatement of the problem, cut him short with, "Yes, that's exactly why I called you in. I do want to talk to you about your carelessness with the cabinets." He will attempt to blur the issue. Your job is to focus, without rancor or hostility, on his *present* mistake, not on his past ones. You must proceed with tact at this early stage, but there is no need to pussyfoot too long if you are dealing with a relatively clear-cut problem.

After saying, "Right. I am concerned about your recent carelessness with the cabinets," you might say quietly, "What happened? You made a mistake that cost us a bundle." At this point, be on your guard. He is well prepared with excuses for why it wasn't his fault. It is important for you to cut off excuses by saying pleasantly, "Just tell me what happened." If he doesn't give you a clear-cut explanation of what he did that caused the problem, become quite specific. Ask a few questions that focus on the current problem, such as, "What did the customer specify?" or "Was it in writing?" or "Did the customer sign off on the final layout?" Your objective is to get the real story without a lot of emotional flak. John will be forced by your approach to focus on his present behavior.

Even at Step 2 of RPM you will be aware that something has changed from your usual discussions with John. Instead of becoming defensive and giving a lot of excuses, he will talk to you calmly about the problem. This happens because you did not ask him why he always makes this kind of mistake or why he made three costly errors in the last six months. You are not badgering him with the inadequacy of what he did or why he didn't fill out the installation checklist or how much his past mistakes have cost. You are asking not for reasons but for facts. Although he will try to interject excuses into the discussion, he will be less likely to dwell on them, because you have done nothing to provoke his defensiveness. You have not threatened to punish him. You have, instead, stuck to the specific project that went wrong and found out where it stands in terms of what was ordered and what was done or not done.

While John won't immediately recognize the full impact of your approach, he will recognize that your approach is different and that all you want to do is help him correct the present situation and avoid future mistakes. Furthermore, if you have been supportive in the past, and not sarcastic or punitive, he will quickly perceive that your interest in finding out what didn't get done was not to fault him, but rather to determine whether the facts are amenable to correction. Once he is convinced that the facts will not be used against him, he will be willing, even eager, to put them forward. As you continue, you will be surprised at how openly he will respond to you and how quickly a chronic problem can be brought under control.

Don't Dwell on Feelings—Move to Performance

When discussing a performance problem with an employee it is important that you not dwell on how the person feels about this particular problem, about his or her life, and about the job in general. Instead, direct attention toward getting the problem solved. Of all the things we suggest in this book, playing down feelings and not dwelling on them may be the most difficult for you. In almost every book and course on how to deal with employees, it has been emphasized over and over again that feelings are important, that if you don't understand how your employees feel you cannot help them.

When things go wrong, both the manager and failing employee feel badly. It's natural for the employee to be frustrated, depressed, fearful, or openly hostile. It's equally natural for the boss to be angry and to want to punish the employee for creating unnecessary problems. The trouble is that all these feelings not only don't get the job done but they stand in the way. The more you dwell on, discuss, and bring to the surface these feelings, the less will get done and the more the discussion will descend into a morass of conflicting passions guaranteed to make everyone feel worse.

We do not suggest that you be unresponsive to how people feel. Far from it. RPM is a human approach to handling people and performance problems which is designed to help people feel better. But it is important to take into account two things about feelings which relate to performance: (1) You should not forget that no one can do badly and still feel good. The more you discuss with employees how they feel about what they are doing and why they are doing it, the less they will change. Unless they change, they will never feel good. When they do change they will feel good. This is a fact. Keep it in mind when you talk to an employee about poor performance. (2) Many people use feelings as justification for poor performance, feelings like "I'm not appreciated" or "Nobody listens to me at Acme" or "I do all the work while others sit around" or "Why do you always hassle me?" can act as smoke screens for not doing the job right.

Suppose an employee wants to express some feelings. What should you do? Avoid becoming enmeshed in long, emotional, rationalizing discussions. Accepting that a person has feelings and letting those feelings justify poor performance are two completely different things. The both-win approach to better feelings is to move the discussion along *productive* avenues. You will find the following two techniques helpful:

1. If an employee insists on talking about feelings, listen for as brief a time as possible without openly rejecting what is being said. Then say, "I understand you're upset. Let's take a look at what you are doing and solve the problem." This will redirect attention from problems to opportunities.
2. When people tell you how badly they feel about their work or

their lives, say as quickly as you can, "Would you like to feel better?" This tops the misery and reminds the employee that good feelings are possible. Simply stated, if you must talk about feelings—and sometimes you will have to—don't forget good feelings. As soon as you bring up good feelings, it will be possible to talk about good behavior, and you are on your way to helping the person feel better and perform better.

Let's say that as soon as you brought up the subject of John's carelessness with the cabinets, he launched into an emotional tirade about how he has too much to do at Acme, doesn't get paid enough, has to share a secretary, hasn't got a quiet office to concentrate in, or isn't liked by the production manager. If you are a good listener, he may tell you about his troubles at home, his high mortgage, and the fact that his kid is hanging around with the wrong crowd. You'll be tempted to listen at great length, but don't. Remember you must move John to performance if you want him to feel better. Say quietly and quickly, "Look, John, I appreciate your difficulties, but I think we can work out a way to stop making this kind of mistake. Wouldn't you feel better if we could solve this ridiculous problem?" Then be tough and on target. Don't deviate from this. Don't let him dwell again on his troubles with the organization and his life. If he brings them up, say, "John, you can handle this problem of carelessness. You handle tougher situations than this every day at work and handle them well." Then, move the discussion one step further by saying, "You do believe it's important to avoid these mistakes, don't you?" or "You understand how important it is to get things right?" or "There is one thing we just can't change around here, and that's the need for everybody to be very careful. We have no surplus funds to cover for those who don't."

Now you're ready to put the third step of RPM to work.

RPM STEP 3: HAVE THE EMPLOYEE EVALUATE HIS OR HER OWN PERFORMANCE

If the facts of what the employee is doing have been put on the table, the question of whether or not his or her present performance is helping to solve the problem is usually obvious. At this point in the discussion, employees generally realize that their behavior is not helping, and probably hurting, the situation. For example, if an employee is chronically late and states flatly that being late is good for the company, then the chances of getting much out of this person are slim. On the other hand, the employee may claim that the time is made up by working late. In this case, you may have to explain that his lateness is disruptive and costly and creates communication problems with other employees. What you say may get him to evaluate the situation more realistically and in a broader context.

Suppose that you have a competent employee who is not performing as well as usual but that there are complex factors affecting the performance. In this case, after the facts are on the table, ask this employee in a calm, dispassionate way if what he or she is doing is really helping to get the job done. This requires some skill and a lot of patience. It usually means going through complicated procedures step-by-step and asking the employee for an evaluation of his or her role in the larger project.

Be prepared for the employee to put up a good defense. If this happens—as it often does with competent employees—we suggest that you accept the defense by saying, "OK, I can see your viewpoint. I don't completely agree with it, but I can certainly see the reason for what you are doing. But could I ask you this? Do you believe that there is at least a possibility that what you are doing may not be the best way to handle this particular situation?" Most employees, with an accepting manager, will then say, "Yes, of course, there is a possibility, but I've given this a lot of thought and I think this is the way to go." You then repeat, "Oh, I agree, I understand that. But look, could we for a while try a different way?" Here, of course, you are moving on to Step 4—developing a get-well plan—which we will cover in the next chapter. But what you are trying to do in Step 3 is to get the employee to be open to trying something else that you think will produce better results.

The point here—and we believe this is an important point, especially when dealing with competent employees—is to suggest the experimental approach. Most people refuse to change their ways, unless they can be persuaded that a new approach is a temporary, "let's judge it as we go along" change. It's surprising how many people are open to change if they look at a different procedure as a trial or an experiment. A good manager or supervisor keeps this point in mind. While it may be against human nature to change when we believe we're right, it's also human nature to experiment, to try something new, to be curious about an alternative.

When you suggest an experiment, always suggest it for a certain period of time, and always build in an evaluation procedure. Preface your remarks by saying that the new plan is just an experiment, and you may be wrong, but you would like the employee to take a look at things and make a judgment about the situation. Because you admit the possible fallibility of your suggestion, the employee becomes more involved in the new procedure and has a stake in making it work. If it does work, you will then hear enthusiastic accounts of all the things he or she did to make it work. In effect, your plan becomes a part of the *employee's* approach, rather than something that has been imposed on someone.

Step 3 of RPM, having the employee evaluate his or her own performance, is important in business because most employees will admit that what they are doing is not helping the problem, *but—* and then proceed to give excuses. If you catch yourself arguing with an employee about excuses or whether certain behavior is helping or hurting the situation, you are not following Step 3. Give the person more time to think about how he or she is performing, and wait for a good time to have another conference.

Steps 4 and 5—working with your employee to develop a plan to solve the problem and getting a commitment to it—are the next steps, and they are the core of RPM. Try to get to this point in your discussion as quickly as possible. Remember, if you maintain a caring, supportive attitude and get the facts of the situation without building a defensive barrier between you, the employee will be willing, if not anxious, to get on with the job of doing things right.

5

RPM Steps 4 and 5: Negotiate a "Get-Well" Plan and Obtain a Commitment to the Plan

The essence of our management–human relations approach is that positively directed action, not talk, improves performance and provides lasting satisfaction. This chapter focuses on how manager and employee figure out a better way to solve the problem and commit themselves to that course of action.

So far the discussion has centered on the employee, but in all these RPM steps, responsibility also falls on the manager or supervisor, who must also squarely face what he or she is doing, evaluate it, and then help figure out a better way. This often involves a change in the manager's behavior as well as in the employee's. There is almost always a better way to do any management task or to solve a personal or performance problem.

HOPING FOR THE BEST

Ralph is production manager of the Acme Cabinet Company. Like a lot of other people at Acme, he's got problems, too. Ralph is in his forties and really knows the technical side of manufacturing cabinets. His trouble is that he is a hope-for-the-best manager. Ralph believes in delegating authority just as the management books suggest he should. A very busy man, he wants desperately to unload some responsibility on his employees. This is what happened on the Lacey job, the one that had to be redone because John goofed up on the oven dimensions. Ralph got a little kick out of John's mistake, but he made sure no one at Acme knew how he felt. It served John right, Ralph couldn't help thinking, for all the crazy, hard-to-produce designs John always seems to come up with.

Lacey, the contractor, had been furious at the delay John caused and had threatened to stop doing business with Acme unless the job was redone within three weeks. Ralph knew it was a tight schedule when he promised Ed, the grim-faced manufacturing vice-president, that he would meet it. Ralph immediately wrote out the new work order, checked all the dimensions, and personally dropped it into Charlie's work-order box with a big note in red reading: "Charlie, get to this right away. Highest priority!" How was he to know that Charlie, his best carpenter, would catch a cold and be out for a week? After all, Ralph had twelve other big projects going and over one hundred people in his department. Could anyone be expected to keep track of everyone every day? Besides, Charlie was a good, reliable man.

Two weeks later, when Ralph was on his way to a project status meeting, he met Charlie on the production floor and asked how the job was coming. When Charlie said, "Which job?" Ralph sensed trouble. Patiently, he explained which job. Charlie then said, "Oh, that one. I didn't see your note until four days ago when I returned from being sick. That reminds me, there are a few things I wanted to get straight before I start. I guess you know we're out of those special cedar panels. How much do you want me to order? They take a week or two to deliver." What followed was not printable in the Acme employee newsletter. Ralph was angry with Charlie, and he berated him on the shop floor in front of others, which he knew he shouldn't do. The pity was that Ralph was more angry at himself for not having the good sense to check the job's progress sooner.

That's what happens to people who hope for the best and don't get it. A year of rapport that had been carefully built between Ralph and Charlie was jeopardized because the boss hoped for the best instead of making a specific plan, getting a solid commitment, and following up at critical milestones. Yes, Ralph had hoped that Charlie would get the job done in three weeks. He had hoped that Charlie would let him know if any problems arose along the way. But his hopes weren't answered and neither were the vice-president's. Ed had hoped for the best when he accepted his production manager's schedule promise but never bothered to check its status. When the job was finally completed a month later, it took a lot of talking and some big concessions by Acme's president to save the Lacey account.

The trouble with the hope-for-the-best approach is that it is seductively simple. It's so logical and tempting for the already too busy manager to delegate some responsibility to others. But the reality of the situation is that there is a world of difference between delegating responsibility and getting a job done. If there is one characteristic that separates good managers who plan from poor ones who don't, it is "hoping for the best." The good manager hopes for the best but *does* something to assure the best will happen. The bad manager just hopes and waits for it to happen. More often than not, the poor manager waits in vain, leaving behind a battlefield of unsolved problems and angry, frustrated employees.

To stress the importance of making good plans, we suggest that you now take the quiz at the end of this chapter, "Are You a Hope-for-the-Best Manager?" As you will see from taking the quiz, we all are to some extent prone to hope for the best. Luckily, some things do work out once in a while. But with the employee who has a serious problem or with the marginally competent employee, hoping for the best rarely works. And if you are the hoper, you get aggravated. The aggravation causes you to reject the problem employee or to lecture instead of carefully listening to what is being said. And to reduce irritation, you may fluctuate haphazardly between demanding better performance and ignoring the problem. In either case, the situation gets worse. Step 4 of RPM states that if you want a job done better, you will not succeed unless both you and the employee make a specific plan, commit yourselves to it, and follow up. Hoping for the best is only an invitation to disaster.

RPM STEP 4: NEGOTIATE A "GET-WELL" ACTION PLAN

You have completed RPM Step 3. You and the employee have put the performance problem on the table and have evaluated it. You agree that something must be done. You must now make a "get-well" plan you both can live with. The psychological payoff for making an improvement plan without delay is that employees will recognize that you're not only offering friendly support but that you also have confidence in their ability to improve. Whenever someone in authority conveys through actions and words "I have confidence in you," the other person gains greater self-confidence. But timing is critical. The longer the manager or supervisor delays in negotiating a better plan, the weaker the employee becomes.

Be Specific

What are the ingredients of an improvement plan that will work? The first and most important element is specificity. Generalities lead nowhere. Quickly get down to exactly what it is that will produce something better. Don't be fuzzy or try to tackle too many improvements at once. If you want Bob, the Acme accounts receivable clerk, to improve, it will do no good to ask him to try harder, to promise to do better. What you must do with Bob, *after* patiently going through RPM Steps 1, 2, and 3, is say, "Look, Bob, what you are doing isn't working. You know it and I know it. I would like to take the time right now to figure out a better way."

Bob might well say, "Hey, it's not that big a deal. Don't worry about it. I'll straighten it all out." And here, instead of hoping that he will, you must interject, "Look, Bob, it is a big deal and I am worried about it. Let's talk about what you can do starting tomorrow morning that will get the invoices caught up so that Acme can get paid on time." Be specific. Say, "Bob, tell me exactly what you are going to do tomorrow to catch up on unprepared invoices. Which ones will go out tomorrow and how many will you do per day until you catch up?" Bob may hem and haw and complain that he has too much to do. He may say that he could easily catch up on the invoices in a few days if he had no accounting entries to do or if he were to postpone follow-up on the late payments. What you should do is press Bob to develop a specific "get-well" plan that will take care of the delinquent invoices and maintain for a while a minimally acceptable level on his other deficiencies, such as late accounting entries and payments.

Give-and-take on your part will be necessary to help Bob develop a workable plan, because the problem has gone on for so long. You may have to provide Bob with overtime, extra help, and personal support. The important thing is that you insist on a specific, detailed plan that Bob has a big part in developing and is willing to commit himself to.

After the plan is negotiated, you should agree to milestone checkpoints. You may arrange with Bob that during the next few days you and he will review progress four times a day against specific catch-up goals. As time goes on and the problem abates, checking can be less frequent, but if Bob is to learn self-discipline in working toward a plan, he must be helped to develop this trait in a systematic way. From your standpoint, spending such time with Bob will be a good investment, because he will gain pride and confidence in meeting his commitments. With the strength of a faster-spinning flywheel, Bob will be in a better position to tackle the accounting entry and payment delinquencies. One thing at a time is a good rule for employees who have a number of failings.

Don't be surprised if Bob has a relapse after he has been caught up for a while. If this happens, talk over the situation with him again and offer the same solution. This time, better performance is apt to result even more quickly. You should not treat the relapse as a crisis of broken faith, nor should you overreact to it. With patience, persistence, planning, commitment, and follow-up, Bob will become stronger and more self-responsible.

A workable plan is a *specific* plan, whether the problem to be solved is simple or complex. Here are some points you must be specific about if you want improved performance:

1. Go over the plan in detail so that both of you understand exactly *what* is to be done.
2. Agree specifically on *when* it is to be done. It's not enough to say "soon" or "as soon as possible" or "in three weeks."
3. Specify the *quality* of work you want. "Good work" or "better work" is not a useful standard leading to better performance. Your employee must know what "good" or "bad" means. If you can't describe it, he can't do it.
4. Specify a *quantity* standard for the employee to shoot at. Remarks like "I'd like a little more" or "You seem to be a little slow" just serve to frustrate the employee, who will then be likely to produce less rather than more.

5. Specify review points or milestones at which you and the employee will check progress on the agreed plan. If you want someone to hammer fifteen nails by 2:00 P.M., don't hope for the best. The effective manager checks the second, the seventh, and the tenth nail at specific times of the day to assure that the fifteenth nail will be driven by 2:00 P.M. The inefficient manager discovers at 2:00 P.M. that the employee didn't even have a hammer.

By this time, you will recognize that the essential elements of being specific are the same whether you are working out a contract with a seller or finding a better way for an employee to perform a task. Both require clarity or the job will remain undone.

Get the Employee to Help Make the Plan

Since the best plans benefit both parties, it makes good sense to try to get your employee to participate in developing the plan. The more the employee participates, the more likely he or she will be to follow through. Let's face it, your employee usually knows more about the details of a particular job than you do. If employees perceive that you are behind them, they will often surprise you with how much they really know about the problem and its solution.

The following techniques can guide you in eliciting your employee's knowledge to make a better "get-well" plan. Say to the employee, "Look, you've been working on this project for quite a while. What do you think we ought to do?" Or you might vary this approach and say, "Look, when I was doing your job I had my way of doing it, but I haven't been sitting in your chair for a long time. What do you suggest?" Or say, "Look, I think we're in a rut. We've been doing it this way for years and it's never worked well. I'll bet you've had a better way in mind for quite a while. Am I right?" This latter approach recognizes that the employee does evaluate his or her work and does care. But it also recognizes that many employees are too timid to go against established policy. This opens the door for the employee to give an opinion, and sometimes you'll get a real breakthrough. Too many employees look at their bosses as rubber stamps for company policy, and unless you give them the opening they will never make the suggestion.

Be Realistic

A good plan is also realistic. It has a reasonable chance for success within the agreed-on time and within the competence of the employee. If you are not realistic—and this is a matter of judgment about the job and who's working for you—your plan will fail. A good way to test the reality of a plan is to ask the employee such questions as "Look, is this schedule realistic?" or "Are we dreaming to think that this job can be done in the specified time?" This covers the common situation where you think the goal is realistic and the employee doesn't. Unless there is a meeting of the minds on the goal in the beginning, a lot of time will be wasted along the way. Also remember that if you honestly ask for your employee's opinion, he or she will usually offer to do more than you had in mind, not less. In the long run, letting employees help you set goals will produce much more work than setting them yourself and "assuming" they are in tune with your objectives.

Set Performance Targets

How much performance improvement should you as a manager or supervisor strive for? Initially, you might be apt to answer, "As much as I can get." That answer is right when you're dealing with a highly competent employee, but it's wrong when you're trying to jack up the performance of a relatively marginal or incompetent employee.

With a marginal employee, you should set your goals in the beginning with one view in mind: to build success patterns. This means that even though you believe the employee will eventually perform at a higher level, don't expect immediate results. Aim for just a little bit more work than the employee has been doing, aim for what he or she might succeed in reaching. Success builds on success. You want to get the employee's performance flywheel going so that more will be done in the future. If you aim for goals too far above present competence, the employee will probably fail and thus grow weaker.

If you want a competent performer to do more, don't be afraid to aim high. With such an employee, the basic rule of business negotiation applies: *Aim higher and you will do better.*

There is another—opposite—approach, which is also effective in dealing with both competent and marginal employees and which sometimes produces a remarkable jump in performance. It calls for you, the manager or supervisor, to set unrealistically *low* goals. For example, with a very competent employee, when you want a tough, time-consuming job done as soon as possible and are reluctant to ask for a deadline of Wednesday at 10:00 A.M., you might say, "Look this is very important. When can you get it done?" The employee may reply "When do you want it?" At this point you can say, "Well, it would really help me if you could have it this Wednesday at ten A.M. But I'm not going to ask you to commit yourself to that goal. I mean, there's a heck of a lot of work here. Let's be realistic. I'll take it Friday evening at five P.M., because I just can't see how in the world you could get it done by Wednesday at ten A.M." With this approach, it is likely you'll get it *before* Friday, and with a very competent employee you might get it Wednesday at 10:00 A.M. or even sooner. The employee will be challenged because everybody likes to gain recognition for achieving the impossible. If an employee does achieve the impossible, be sure to take time to provide the recognition that is deserved.

With an incompetent employee, you might also set an unrealistically low goal. You might go so far as to say, "Look, I am not going to set any deadline for this at all. I've set deadlines, we've argued about them, and they haven't worked out. This time I'm just going to wait until you get the job done. Let me know when it's finished." By reversing your usual procedure, you place the responsibility on the employee. He or she can't complain about being hassled by you or about being asked to do too much, and all the usual excuses will be undercut by this unfamiliar request. The longer this employee goofs off, the more nervous he or she will become; it's likely that the work will be done faster than either of you expected. When the job is completed say, "Gee, that's good. How did you get it done so quickly?" This approach must be used judiciously. When you do use it, you must keep an eye on how things are going.

RPM STEP 5: GET A RESPONSIBLE EMPLOYEE COMMITMENT TO THE PLAN

Without a commitment to make them succeed, the best-laid plans are often doomed to failure. Therefore, it is crucial to get your employee committed to the "get-well" plan. Too often we take commitment for granted and overlook this simple step. If you have spent considerable time working out a plan in some detail, it makes sense to spend a few more minutes to secure a commitment from your employee that he or she will put the plan into action.

Commitment may be signified by a simple handshake, solid eye contact following a verbal agreement, or a firm declaration from the employee, "I'm going to do it and you can count on it." Commitment need not be a big, formal deal, but the more definite it is, the more chance that plan will be carried out.

A time element should be part of most commitments. Ask, "When can we expect the job to be completed?" and agree on a time. Establish with your employee the understanding that commitments can be renegotiated, but don't be open-ended about it. Work is not open-ended but rather discrete time intervals, such as Friday afternoon at 2:00 P.M. or next Tuesday at 10:00 A.M. Getting a firm commitment takes time on your part, but it is an essential element in good supervision.

Even when a plan seems quite workable, you might sometimes want to get a written commitment. Bankers, lawyers, and car salespersons all want you to sign on the dotted line, even when they know that you are a good credit risk. They know that things can happen between a handshake and the payment, so they cement the agreement by asking for your signature. With many employees securing a written, signed commitment to the plan makes good sense. Keep a copy and give them a copy.

If you are dealing with a very recalcitrant employee whom you are considering terminating, getting a written, signed commitment may be essential. If things don't work out, you have protected yourself from a lot of disagreeable misunderstandings. This is just the kind of employee who will say to you, "Well, I never really thought that's what I had to do" or "You never made it clear" or "This is the first I've heard that you really wanted that much." When this occurs, just take out the written agreement, read it, and say, "Is there anything here that you didn't understand when you signed it? It certainly seemed clear when we went over it a week ago."

We would like to reemphasize that what goes on between you and your employees is a human relationship, regardless of the business context. Employees know that they are going to get paid. They know the work rules and the industry regulations, and they probably know pretty well how to do their jobs. What they don't know is whether or not you support them. This is where a mutual commitment is so meaningful. Commitment is the essence of any strong human relationship, and it makes the time spent between you and your employees even more valuable.

We have all seen people suffer because of a lack of commitment. They are always worried that if they commit themselves, something may come along and cause them to regret the bargain they made. They are reluctant to stay on this side of the fence because the other side might be greener. They spend their lives hopping back and forth over fences rather than settling down on one side and doing the job. Securing commitments from employees is good for them, because it provides them with the security of knowing that they have a workable plan and a boss who believes in them and supports them.

When you ask an employee for a commitment, you solidify your relationship. You are telling those who work for you, "I care about you, I care about what you do, and I care for your sake and mine that you get it done." Every organization needs commitment from its employees, and the more the better. Commitment means we won't spend our time figuring out why we can't do a job. It means that we believe in one another and that we are strong enough to get the job done. Commitment to one another means that we are not alone, that we can call on others for help. This simple step of agreeing to a "get-well" plan and asking for and receiving a commitment to follow through will result in a surprising amount of performance improvement.

WHAT TO DO IF THE PLAN DOESN'T WORK

Sometimes, in spite of all the good intentions and commitments, a plan doesn't work out. Then the plan must be renegotiated. You must come up with a new course of action. Notice we did not mention discussing with the employee *why* the plan didn't work. We will discuss that in Step 6, when we talk about not accepting any excuses. For now, we will assume that there are valid reasons why the plan didn't work and that a modified plan or a new plan is needed. Do not spend time analyzing why the plan did not work, lamenting its failure, or finding fault and placing blame. Instead, try to develop a better, perhaps more imaginative and creative plan that will work. As soon as possible, get to "What do we have to do to make it work and when can we do it?" The words "what" and "when" are good RPM words that teach the employee to move ahead. They are much more effective than the natural excuse-getter "why."

Good managers realize they don't know why some plans don't work. In fact, the person who knows the most about how to solve the problem is the employee, who at this point seems stuck. We emphasize *seems* stuck, because in many cases employees are not stuck but only say so to get some recognition. They are worried that if they solve the problems too easily they will not get the credit for the solution they believe they deserve. It's natural to want recognition, and if they solve problems, give them the recognition they deserve. The manager's job is not to worry about who gets credit but to get the job done. If you don't find a way to call on your employees' ingenuity, you will discover that very often they are not going to offer it.

It is common for an employee to like to see the boss "sweat," to "really earn his money for a change." If you are the kind of manager who barks orders rather than renegotiating, those who work for you will offer little or nothing when they see you in trouble. Ask their opinions and listen to what they say, and you'll be surprised how many problems can get solved.

Even in the extreme case when an employee says "There is no way this can be done" and you look the job over and don't see a way either, you may still be able to elicit a solution to the problem. The employee has given you a flat "This is it," but instead of accepting such a non-negotiable position you might say, "I don't think there is a way either, but I am going to turn you loose and give you nothing to do for a couple of hours (or days, if the problem is complex) except work at this problem. I'll be open to almost anything you suggest." Under these circumstances, when you express this kind of confidence in their initiative, you'll be surprised at how creative many people become. Remember that the psychological roots of creativity and success come from a deep belief in oneself. When people who are important express confidence in you, you get an immediate burst of self-confidence. Areas of your brain which were previously closed become open, working, and clear.

For example, while Dr. Glasser was remodeling his house, the plumber came to him and said, "You know the small bathroom on the first floor behind the den? I can't put a toilet in it." "How can there be a bathroom without a toilet?" Dr. Glasser asked. The plumber just shrugged and said, "There's no way I can put this toilet in, because the cement man goofed." The implication was that the cement would have to be jackhammered out and repoured to get the toilet in. Realizing that many subcontractors don't do the work exactly to specifications, but realizing, too, that the houses they work on get built and function, Dr. Glasser said, "How long have you been plumbing?" "Twenty-five years," the plumber answered. "Do you consider yourself a good plumber?" "I sure do." "In your twenty-five years as a plumber, have you ever run into a problem as difficult as this?" He laughed. "Sure, lots of times." "OK," said Dr. Glasser, "then put in the toilet and don't bother me." The toilet was put in. The plumber had been asking for a vote of confidence. He wanted his employer to know how difficult his job was, and he wasn't about to put the toilet in and let anyone assume it was just an ordinary installation.

Perhaps another example is the mile run. The world's record keeps dropping, and people now talk seriously about a 3½-minute mile when most of us still remember the miracle of the 4-minute mile. Will we get a 3½-minute mile? Probably. Why will we get it? Because someone will develop enough strength and self-confidence to strive for the impossible and achieve it.

What managers and supervisors should be trying to do is turn loose this capability within employees to get them to say to themselves, "There's no reason why I can't do it." If we criticize and carp, we'll hear every reason why they can't, and they won't. But if you build confidence in your employees through these RPM steps, through a good plan and through commitment to that plan, "can't" will become an obsolete word in your organization.

Before we get too enthusiastic about how to improve performance dramatically, let's come down to earth and face the fact that some jobs just can't be done. And for economic or other reasons, some impediments cannot be removed. You don't want to push your employees to the point they believe that "can't" is never an acceptable answer. They will think you have lost touch with reality. When the job simply can't be done or when real impediments cannot be removed, if you have good rapport both of you will recognize it is impossible. Make a rational, unemotional plan for *how to live with the situation* as it is, and go on to other things. Don't get hung up on what can't be done. Always move your flywheel toward performance.

ARE YOU A HOPE-FOR-THE-BEST MANAGER?

This quiz is for your information only. Don't reveal your score to anyone. Circle the number along the scale that best represents your normal response to situations.

1. Do you periodically and systematically spot-check your department to keep abreast of what is really going on?

Rarely   Always
1   2   3   4   5   6

2. Do you tend to be specific about when you want a job done, for example, March 3 at 10:00 A.M.?

Rarely   Always
1   2   3   4   5   6

3. Do you assume that what you think is the trouble and what your employee thinks is the trouble are the same?

Usually   Rarely
1   2   3   4   5   6

4. Are you meticulous about understanding the details of the contracts you sign?

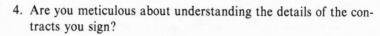

Rarely   Almost Always

1   2   3   4   5   6

5. Do you take the time to be specific and precise about what you want done?

Rarely   Almost Always

1   2   3   4   5   6

6. Do you assume that your employees trust that you have their welfare in mind even though you give them very little time?

Usually   Rarely

1   2   3   4   5   6

7. Do you follow up on your progress milestones as the job is being done?

Rarely   Almost Always

1   2   3   4   5   6

8. When hiring an employee and requesting three former supervisors as references, do you check all three?

Rarely   Usually

1   2   3   4   5   6

9. Do you work your assignments out so that progress can be easily followed while the work is being done?

Rarely   Almost Always

1   2   3   4   5   6

10. Do you tend to be specific about how much you want done?

Rarely   Almost Always

|———————|———————|———————|———————|———————|

1   2   3   4   5   6

11. Do you tend to assume that your employees will soon get over feeling badly after you become involved in a long heated emotional discussion about what they did wrong?

Usually   Rarely

|———————|———————|———————|———————|———————|

1   2   3   4   5   6

12. Do you assume that your employees will openly and promptly let you know when things go wrong?

Usually   Rarely

|———————|———————|———————|———————|———————|

1   2   3   4   5   6

13. After you spend a lot of time finding out why a job wasn't completed and/or whose fault it was, do you tend to assume that once both of you know what happened it won't happen again?

Usually   Rarely

|———————|———————|———————|———————|———————|

1   2   3   4   5   6

14. Do you tend to assume that the problem employee is automatically committed to do the task when you assign a job?

Usually   Rarely

|———————|———————|———————|———————|———————|

1   2   3   4   5   6

15. Do you actively pursue a program to create good working relationships with other departments, or do you let it work itself out without special attention?

Little Attention   Active Program

|———————|———————|———————|———————|———————|

1   2   3   4   5   6

16. Do you assume that your carefully designed procedures are being followed because they are well understood and are of recognized importance to all?

Usually   Rarely

1   2   3   4   5   6

17. When you make plans, do you leave enough room for things to go wrong?

Rarely   Almost Always

1   2   3   4   5   6

18. When you give a competent employee an important assignment outside his area of competence, do you rarely check his progress carefully because he usually does such a fine job?

Rarely Check   Always Check

1   2   3   4   5   6

19. When a problem has been corrected, do you then tend to assume all will go well in the future?

Usually   Rarely

1   2   3   4   5   6

20. Do you tend to be careful when selecting competent professional advice (e.g., accounting, legal, medical, engineering, architecture, skilled tradespeople)?

Rarely   Almost Always

1   2   3   4   5   6

Scoring

Total the circled numbers for the twenty questions. If your score is 95 or more, you are a better manager than most of us. If your score is between 20 and 45, you are hoping for too much and have a lot to gain by following the advice in this chapter. Take the quiz again in three months and compare results.

6

RPM Step 6: Don't Accept Excuses, Move to Performance

Don't become involved with excuses when employees fail to meet their commitments. Learn to avoid asking "Why is it late?" or "What went wrong?" When excuses are offered, don't fall into the traps of listening too long or, even worse, accepting the excuse. Learn to say without anger, even with some compassion but with a great deal of firmness, "Look, I'm much less interested in what went wrong than in *when* you will have it. What is our present plan of action?"

Because we are human, RPM Step 6, don't accept excuses but move to performance, is probably the most difficult step. It seems that as our world grows more complex we spend more and more time figuring out *why* things can't be done instead of *how* to do them. Too often we appear to operate on the assumption that if there is a good enough excuse the job need not be done or need not be done well. At Acme Cabinet Company that's exactly the problem that Ed, the manufacturing vice-president, has. Whenever things go wrong, he always tells the president that it's not his fault, and it isn't; it's always the fault of someone else.

When at the project status meeting, Ed told the president that the Lacey cabinet job would be another three weeks late, the president blew his cool. "Ed," he said almost sarcastically, "tell me what went wrong this time." Well, Ed told him everything that went wrong. It was all beyond his control. He went through the designer's mistake, Charlie's absence, and Ralph's failure to follow up as he should have. Then he dumped the problem on the president. The reason there were no cedar panels in inventory was Acme's cash-flow problem. The president had personally ordered that all cedar inventories were to be kept low because Bob had screwed up in accounts receivable and failed to invoice and collect from customers.

Before long, everyone at the meeting was shouting—Ed, Ralph, the president, and the controller who had hired Bob. Then they formed a committee to study the matter. Acme's president had asked Ed for reasons why the job hadn't gotten done, and that's what Ed delivered—lots of reasons and excuses. At Acme there was never a shortage of reasons why things couldn't get done.

We are so surrounded by excuse-givers that at times we are amazed when someone says they'll do something tough and then actually follows through and does it. Even with people we deal with frequently, we expect that promises will be broken as often as they are kept. Unfortunately, the more we accept excuses from others, the more we start to depend too much on excuses ourselves. As we listen over and over again to why this or that wasn't done, our accepting attitude encourages a host of interesting "good reasons" for what went wrong. Slowly but surely we begin to make excuses part of our own repertoire. But excuses, good or bad, don't get the job done. So, in Step 6 of RPM we recommend firmly that you *don't ask for, don't give, and don't accept excuses.*

At this point many readers may wonder how we can live without excuses. "They just didn't deliver the material." "The factory burned down." "There was a flood." "Have you forgotten the blizzard?" "It was stolen." "They've been on strike." "The bank was closed." "The check's in the mail." "Your line has been busy all afternoon." "You didn't really mean Tuesday at ten o'clock, did you?" To deal with these and many more of our oldest and dearest excuse friends, we offer the RPM law that states, *"Every excuse is a good excuse."*

Try to think of a time when you failed to do something and didn't offer an excuse. And try to think of a time when your good excuse was not accepted or didn't make any difference in terms of not getting the job done. Every excuse has the same purpose: to relieve the person of responsibility for not performing. Since we all use excuses, we tend to accept them too readily. But now ask yourself how many times your excuse made you stronger and more likely to succeed in the future. The trouble with excuses is that they drastically interfere with commitment; they dilute it, and by diluting your employee's commitment, you weaken ability, initiative, and planning. The employee will work less and alibi more.

No excuse ever got a job done, so why waste time talking or arguing about whether the excuse is good or bad? Navy Admiral Hyman Rickover, who got the Polaris nuclear submarine built against severe odds, could have said to those under his command, "But nobody told me there would be so many problems." Instead, he said, "If there are problems, we'll deal with them and not wonder or argue about where they all came from." Rickover got the submarine built in a time of great potential danger.

THE PAYOFF FOR NOT ACCEPTING EXCUSES

Even if you follow the assumption that excuses don't get the job done, you might still argue that it doesn't hurt at least to listen to employees explain "why." We say that it *does* hurt, because when excuses are asked for and accepted, the first thought that occurs to employees is "If I don't get it done, all I need is a good excuse." If employees do not get a job done and you follow Step 6 of RPM without asking for or accepting excuses, the employees will work harder, be more creative in approaching the work, or become much more realistic about how much they claim they can do and the things to which they commit themselves. The payoff is obvious. The more we can get our employees into the no-excuse habit, the more their performances will improve.

To make this policy work, we must not only refuse to listen to excuses, but we must show that we mean what we say by not using excuses ourselves. As in all the steps of RPM, we must practice what we preach. When an employee says, "I want to tell you why it didn't happen," the no-excuse manager should say, "No. Please don't tell me why it didn't happen. Tell me when it is going to happen." This can be said in a warm, compassionate, encouraging way. There need be nothing cold or rejecting about not accepting excuses. Your expectation is: *Get it to happen. Don't tell me why it didn't happen.*

The more this is done, the more employees will learn not to depend on excuses as crutches for nonperformance. Instead of telling you why something couldn't be done, they will learn to start talking about what can be done, how it can be done, and when it will be done. As this policy begins to prevail, employees will become strong enough to get the job done by anticipating and circumventing the obstacles that are always there.

The no-excuse approach strengthens the employee even when an excuse is valid, because it focuses on performance. Suppose when you reject an excuse and say, "When is it going to happen?" the employee says, "The way things are, it just isn't going to happen." You realize that the employee is right; the plan is unrealistic and, the way things are, the job isn't going to get done. An effective manager would then say, "OK. Then what *can* we do to get the job done?" Your no-excuse employee might say, "I need more help and time," and because you are dealing with a competent person you say, "OK. How much more help and how much more time do you need?" Here, if the employee wants to justify why more help and time is needed, you might listen briefly. But if he or she is competent, quickly get to the point by moving back to Step 4, negotiating a new plan, and moving quickly toward a realistic way to get the problem solved. By following the no-excuse approach of Step 6, you generate a can-do philosophy with your subordinates.

Let's take another example. You and your district salesman were scheduled to meet with an important customer in Chicago and your salesman didn't make the meeting. When he finally arrives he greets you with, "I'm sorry. The plane had engine trouble and I was delayed in Saint Louis." Your pre-RPM approach to this situation might have been to engage in a discussion with the employee about all the times people have been delayed by faulty planes. We recognize that being sympathetic to an employee is important, but in terms of getting the job done we ask whether there is any difference between the plane's having had engine trouble and the plane's being missed. In both cases, an important sales opportunity was jeopardized. And, in both cases, something has to be done to solve the problem regardless of the excuses.

Suppose instead of discussing the recurring problem of faulty transportation you say to your salesman, "I know you got here as soon as you could. What can we do to make up for your absence?" You will be exactly where you were with the excuse, but you have quickly moved to solve the problem. We recognize that engine trouble can't be remedied, but we also recognize that in the real world more people are late because they have missed planes than because of engine trouble. Most employees who are treated this way will be much less likely to miss the plane in the future.

Each time you use the no-excuse, move-to-performance approach your employees grow stronger. Try practicing it on small problems as well as large ones. When employees operate in a no-excuse work environment, they will spend their time making things happen instead of dillydallying over why things went wrong.

HOW TO PUT THE NO-EXCUSE, MOVE-TO-PERFORMANCE APPROACH TO WORK

Try to incorporate the following strategies into your relationships with employees:

- Avoid asking, "Why wasn't it done?" All you will get for your trouble are emotional responses that lead to a heated argument.
- Avoid a discussion about what should have been done. Second-guessing may make you feel better, but it won't change what happened.
- When you assign a task, be sure to build in some review points. Check on programs before things go wrong. In this way you will automatically eliminate many excuses.
- Don't ask your employees to bite off more than they can chew. When they make a commitment to do a job, avoid future excuses by saying, "I don't want you to give me an excuse if the job isn't done. Let's make sure this is what you can do before you commit yourself to doing it." Then, if the agreed-upon task doesn't get done, you have already set the tone for refusing to accept an excuse if one is offered.

All the above strategies have one thing in common. They are performance-oriented. They deal exclusively with finding a better way rather than with looking for what went wrong.

Conclusion

Not accepting excuses may seem to be a hard-nosed, tough way of managing. It is, but if it's done with respect, with an "I have confidence in you," "I care about you," and "How can I help you?" approach, excuses will tend to melt away. Without excuses, work proceeds more smoothly among confident, committed people who care something about one another and about what they are trying to do.

We recognize that Step 6 may seem difficult at first, but we believe that as you grow more skillful in the RPM technique there will be a noticeable jump in your effectiveness as a manager and supervisor. The increased spin this adds to your flywheel will make it easier for you to deal with problems in the future.

7

RPM Step 7: Let Natural Consequences Take Over—Don't Punish or Put Down

At times even the best of employees fails to meet an objective or to perform adequately. While you should discuss this failure, no good manager would threaten the employee or be punitive. But with the worker who consistently fails to perform, the temptation you feel to be punitive is both natural and strong. It is, however, the wrong approach to improving performance.

The Judeo-Christian ethic by which our culture tends to abide holds that if you do wrong you should be punished, unless you have a good excuse. If we eliminate excuses, however, it follows that we must find a better way to deal with employees than to punish them when they fail to perform. Excuses abound in a punitive atmosphere, but if we eliminate the threat of punishment and allow people to suffer the natural or reasonable consequences of their own behavior, there will be little or no need for excuses. This important step of RPM is the path toward increased employee self-responsibility.

THE IMPORTANT DIFFERENCE BETWEEN PUNISHMENT AND NATURAL CONSEQUENCES

The big difference between punishing people and letting them suffer the natural consequences of their behavior is that in punishing people you personally put them down and almost always hurt them irretrievably. Allowing employees to suffer the natural consequences of their behavior can also be painful, but it is never personally directed at reducing their self-esteem. The difference is subtle but all-important in its effect on a person's future behavior.

Just because we advocate no punishment does not mean that the RPM way of handling people is soft or ineffective. When you begin to use RPM, you will discover that it is much more tough-minded than the punitive approach, because it puts a premium on responsibility. Employees who fail to perform and do not get a pay increase can still get an increase if they start to perform; the natural consequences of their behavior move them toward responsibility. Too many managers and supervisors are critical, disparaging, or sarcastic when employees fail to perform. In addition to not giving them raises, they also hurt employees by putting them down; they prefer to hurt rather than take the time to teach a better way. Hurting people never fails to make them resentful; it always creates in them a put-down frame of mind from which they rarely have the inclination or strength to learn a better way.

PUNITIVE APPROACHES TO AVOID

Avoid using the following punitive approaches with your employees.

- Ridiculing
- Talking to others about their deficiencies
- Paying no attention to them or their suggestions
- Talking behind their backs
- Leaving them out of social situations, for example, avoiding going to lunch with them
- Picking on their appearance, dress, religion, or race
- Not listening to them
- Demeaning them through a glance or a snide remark
- Giving them demeaning assignments
- Checking on them like children
- Berating and demeaning them in front of others (this is the worst approach of all)

Think about this list. How many times have you treated a problem employee in one or more of these ways? These kinds of approaches have never worked and never will. At best, they discourage employees; at worst, they make enemies out of them. And, as Ben Franklin said, "There's no such thing as a small enemy." Being a good manager is hard enough without antagonizing the people who work for you.

Instead of punishing employees, consider the following as legitimate natural consequences of poor performance:

- No raise
- No promotion
- Termination
- Reduction in assignment scope or responsibility
- Transfer
- No bonus
- Temporary reduction in salary
- Temporary loss of fringe benefits such as use of the company car, gasoline, credit cards, executive lunch room, special parking place, or privileged stock purchases
- Temporary curtailment of such freedoms as making personal calls, getting a haircut, or cashing checks on company time, or taking a few hours off for personal business.

Many readers will argue that failure to give an employee a raise or promotion is punitive, even if we label it a natural or reasonable consequence. We admit that it's tough and often painful for an employee to be denied a raise, but it is not truly punitive because *we have done nothing personally to demean the subordinate* and *what we have done is not irretrievable.* The employee can eventually get the raise or promotion if he or she earns it, but we can never retrieve a sarcastic remark or a put-down. Furthermore, if the remedy to the natural consequences employees temporarily suffer is discussed with honesty, warmth, support, and hope, they may soon gain the strength to get their raises and even to make up more than they lost.

When a person doesn't perform, we don't punish. Instead, we move back to Step 4 and negotiate a new plan that will help the employee do a more competent job and thereby enjoy the positive consequences that go with good performance. With inadequate employees, this may take a while, but at least it sets the stage for them to try. Punishment would cause them to give up or encourage them to justify their resentment and engage in a series of counter-productive activities, thereby making the situation even worse.

While the RPM management way is tough, it always assumes that employees have more control over their performance than they are willing to admit. We want them to exercise that control and to understand that if they do a poor job they have to accept responsibility for their performance. But we want them to understand as well that when they do a good job they will reap the rewards of good performance.

Remember, as damaging and ineffective as it is to put employees down personally, it is just as positive and effective to build them up personally. We encourage you to pat them on the back, to shake their hands, to look them in the eye and tell them they've done a good job. The goal is not to become impersonal but to be personal only on the positive—not the negative—side.

Good managers and supervisors don't avoid employees when the natural consequences of their performance dictate that they receive no raise or promotion. Managers don't become unavailable, mysterious, or curt. They take a short but uninterrupted period of time to give their truthful opinions about the behavior that resulted in no raise or promotion. In talking to employees, good managers do not forget to discuss employees' strong points and to try and solve the problem through an extension of these strengths rather than dwelling upon weaknesses. The big difference between punishing employees and allowing them to suffer the natural consequences of their behavior is that punishment tears people down. Natural consequences make it possible, even likely, that employees will grow.

HOW TO GIVE CONSTRUCTIVE CRITICISM

Every manager and supervisor has found it necessary at one time or another to criticize an employee. If the manager doesn't handle this correctly, the problem will become worse instead of better. One of the most difficult managerial skills to learn is how to criticize people without putting them down or punishing them.

Criticism can be harmful much more than helpful. It causes people to lose confidence in themselves and thereby weakens them. Study the following list of dos and don'ts carefully. It will help you to criticize people in a constructive fashion rather than slowing down or shattering their flywheels.

The Don'ts

- Never criticize employees for what happened in the past.
- Don't criticize anything that can't be changed.
- Don't hurt or demean the other person in any way, even subtly.
- Never criticize subordinates in front of others. If you must do it, talk to them in private. Pick the time and place carefully.

The Dos

- If you must criticize employees recognize that it will slow down their flywheels. Be prepared to give more of your time and support to compensate for the loss of spinning strength and confidence. Get closer.
- Ask yourself before you criticize, "Will my criticism help this person succeed or will it reinforce the feeling of failure?"
- Instead of criticizing, learn to say, "I think we can work out a better way." This builds the employee's strength and implies hope for the future.
- Show the other person the right way. Don't waste time talking about the wrong way.
- Build from the employee's strengths. It is always beneficial to talk about what the other person does right while engaging in constructive criticism. Don't take the person's positive accomplishments for granted.
- Remember that people usually criticize themselves—perhaps too much—when things go wrong. Excessive self-criticism is destructive. A good manager helps employees stop excessive self-criticism.
- The next time you are ready to criticize someone, think about the last big mistake *you* made. It will soften your criticism.

Remember that people want to learn a better way from someone who genuinely wants to help them. Before you start criticizing an employee, ask yourself whether it may be wiser in this instance to let the situation pass without *any* criticism or discussion. Criticism tends to be overdone, just as praise can be underdone.

8

RPM Step 8: Don't Give Up on Employees Too Easily

Managers and supervisors live in a tough, real world. They have to do something with employees who aren't shaping up. While there are times when they will terminate employees, in most cases today termination is not an immediate consideration. Sometimes it's not even possible. Therefore, don't give up too quickly on people who can't be terminated, because the longer they stay in this limbo of knowing they have been given up on, the harder it will be to rehabilitate them.

Let's consider termination first. If nothing works, even the steps of RPM, then we advise termination. However, even if you terminate someone you have an obligation to talk with that person, at least briefly, to try to help him or her make a reasonable plan for the future. This is still a time to show personal acceptance of the employee, at least to the extent of saying, "Look, you didn't do the job here. This doesn't mean you can't do a job somewhere else. Let's take a look at some things you might work on to help yourself in the future." Try to get the employee to open up, and then offer some suggestions. At this point the employee may listen and look to you for advice and friendship. You have an obligation to try to leave the employee with some feeling of self-worth that can be put to work in another situation.

In most cases today, however, termination will not be at issue. It is a fact that in most large industrial or government organizations, you must work with people who for a long time have not performed up to standard. *Your job as a manager or supervisor is to try to negotiate the slippery ground of accepting them as people but not accepting their inadequate performance.* While this is hard to do, if you can do it, you can eventually get such employees to follow through on a plan to perform better.

Many people, long before anything even remotely approaching termination occurs, will frustrate you to the point where you want to give up. This is especially true if you are very busy. One of the differences between good managers and poor managers is that good managers don't give up easily. They recognize that people who show promise can, with effort and a little ingenuity, be helped to blossom into key employees. But we also recognize that any manager must use judgment in determining how much effort to put into what seems to be a losing situation. Therefore, when we say you shouldn't give up, what we really mean is you should hang on and work with poor performers longer than they expect.

Employees who are performing poorly *expect* you to give up on them. Chances are they have had bosses give up on them in the past. When they expect you to give up and you don't, this is often the difference that transmits that extra bit of strength, care, and concern that can turn such employees around. When someone in authority persists in believing in you, it shows a measure of confidence that's very hard for even an incompetent employee to refuse.

You have probably had employees transferred to you who make you want to give up as soon as you meet them. In many cases, your first impression was right. All further effort was wasted. The employee couldn't cut it, and there was nothing you could do. Our advice, however, is to distrust first impressions, even second impressions, and by the time your third impression comes into focus, you may see your employee in a much more positive light. Keep in mind that a good manager judges employees first by the work they do and second by how they get along with others. Beyond this, everything else runs a poor third. Start new employees off on a clean slate and hang in with them a little longer than they expect you to. The payoff is often remarkable.

Suppose you cannot terminate an employee and you have tried unsuccessfully to motivate this employee to do a competent job. What then? Here we advise a last-resort technique that should not be used lightly or frequently but that may motivate someone for the very first time. Call the employee into your office when you have time and say something like this: "Look, I don't know what to do. I have tried everything I know, and with you nothing seems to work. I would just like to tell you that for all practical purposes I have given up. If you have any ideas, this is the last time I'll listen to them. I would like to help you, but truthfully I don't know what to do, and I'm not going to waste any more time."

This approach may startle incompetent or stubborn employees into taking a hard look at things. Suddenly it flashes through their minds that they are really not doing anything and that they're not helping themselves either. Meanwhile, here is another person who, with some kindness and some compassion but a great deal of candor, is saying, "Look, I haven't got the faintest idea how to get you moving." There's no need to talk about termination or threaten them in any way. They know that poor performance has negative consequences. What you are trying to do is appeal to a part of them that suddenly feels lonely and isolated. The boss, who should be resentful, punitive, and rejecting, honestly puts the cards on the table and says, "I don't know what to do."

To repeat, we don't advise using this technique frequently, but when you are absolutely in a bind, it's a way to go that may work when nothing else will.

In a sense, Step 8 of RPM—don't give up easily—summarizes all our steps, because RPM is an approach that keeps trying. We believe you should never give up on being warm, friendly, and human when you work with people. We believe you should be dogged in getting the facts of the present performance on the table and equally resistant to delving into the past or engaging in long, emotional discussions. You should try consistently to get employees to evaluate their own performances in relation to the facts and as quickly as possible move from their evaluation to a better "get-well" plan. If it's important enough to plan, it's important enough to get a commitment to stick to the plan. We advise you not to waste time with excuses, not to be punitive, and, when things go wrong, to be willing to go back again and again to Step 4, renegotiating and refining a better and better plan until things do go right. If you work this way, not giving up is a big part of the way you as a manager are. And it will be a big part of the way your employees will work for you.

Now that the eight steps of RPM have been laid out, you may be wondering what happened at Acme Cabinet Company. Did they ever straighten out, or are they still handling their personnel and performance problems the wrong way? We've got good news and bad news to report. Acme hired a first-rate person to help develop their managers. That's the good news. The bad news is that the person is spending all the time in the field training installers how to correct faulty cabinet work.

What Acme should be doing is having their managers and supervisors follow the eight steps of RPM:

Step 1 - Establish a Supportive Rapport
Step 2 - Get the Facts on the Table Without Going Into the Past or Eliciting Emotional Responses
Step 3 - Let the Employees Evaluate Their Own Performances
Step 4 - Negotiate a "Get-Well" Plan
Step 5 - Obtain a Firm Commitment
Step 6 - Don't Accept Excuses, Move to Performance
Step 7 - Don't Punish or Put Down, Let Natural Consequences Take Over
Step 8 - Don't Give Up on People Easily

9

The Big "Little" Problems of Management: Excessive Lateness, Absenteeism, and Work Breaks

Many managers and supervisors would say that there are no little problems in management, that any problem that reduces productive effort and takes up managerial time is a big problem. Nevertheless, as we talk with managers all over the country, it becomes apparent that there are some irritating problems we should address which are not considered large or important. They are the daily irritants, the upsets that shouldn't crop up but do. Because they tend to be seen as relatively minor and not too important to the overall scheme of things, managers often deal with them haphazardly, instead of using the steps of RPM outlined in the previous chapters.

These "little" problems include lateness, absenteeism, sloppiness, forgetfulness, excessive time off during the day for conversations at the water fountain, the coffee machine, or on the telephone to personal friends. In most organizations, a lot of time is lost and a lot of work is diluted because these problems exist. Collectively, they destroy the discipline and communication that are so necessary to profitable, effective performance.

We recently discussed these matters with a tough-minded manager who stated flatly that if an employee is tardy or absent on a regular basis, it is as much a reflection on the manager as on the employee. His point was that good managers don't allow this to happen—they terminate such employees. We say that the job the employee is doing is usually good enough that letting him or her go would probably cost the company even more time, money, and managerial effort.

Of course, an employee who is flagrantly absent, tardy, unproductive, or sloppy should be terminated. But when? Certainly you don't terminate when the problem first appears; instead, you try to solve it. The RPM approach is a good way to handle people whom you want to help, whether their deficiencies are complex or simple. In this chapter we'll discuss the problem of lateness as a model for some of the other big "little" difficulties that most managers and supervisors face.

From a moral standpoint, any time employees aren't there when they are supposed to be, they are taking something from the company. One of the memorable lines in Charles Dickens' *A Christmas Carol* is Scrooge complaining that Cratchit stole a half-day's wages from him every Christmas when he insisted on going home at one o'clock instead of putting in a full day's work. Scrooge let him go, but he never failed to begrudge him the time off and to remind him that he was picking Scrooge's pocket. We've come a long way since Scrooge, but basically employees who are not working when they should be are removing funds from their employer, raising the cost of goods sold, and making the company less competitive.

Managers are on sound moral grounds in dealing firmly with such matters. Despite this, as RPM Step 1 suggests, it is important that they maintain friendly, supportive working relationships with employees. They should talk with them and compliment them when something good has been done. They should not contact them only when there is a complaint or an inefficiency. Good managers try their best to establish a spirit of comradery and to some extent make work enjoyable. These reflections of care and concern smooth the way for behavioral change when things go wrong.

When a new worker comes aboard, it is essential that the supervisor personally convey the importance of following the ground rules that have to do with lateness, absenteeism, and excessive time away from the work station. This should be done whether the employee is newly hired or a transfer. One manager we know does this by giving each new person a small card that reads: "Obviously you know these rules. You accept the rules or you wouldn't be working here. Nevertheless, it's important as you start with me that you understand these rules are important and should not be broken, unless we discuss that there is a better way than to follow them."

Suppose you are dealing with an employee who has recently been late for work twice. If you do not want this lateness to become chronic, you should not wait to talk it over. The longer you wait, the more difficult it will be. It's not good to have a rule that isn't enforced, and it's not good to wait to enforce a rule. Therefore, any time an employee is late more than once in any month you should deal with the situation promptly.

The initial discussion should be brief. If a good relationship has been established, you should come right to the point: "I'm concerned about your lateness." Don't pussyfoot, don't make this a time for pats on the back and then come up with the subject of lateness. There should be little or no discussion, and you should make it clear that you are not going to spend a great deal of time discussing something as simple as lateness. It is the employee's responsibility to be at work on time, and the manager is merely going to call attention to it. For example, after the employee comes in and pleasantries have been exchanged, you should say, "Last Monday and Thursday you were an hour late for work." The employee may immediately counter with an excuse, but, following RPM Step 6, you should say, "You don't have to give an excuse. I'm sure you had a reason to be late." (Remember what we said about excuses in chapter 7, every excuse is a good excuse.) "All I want to know is whether you understand that work begins at nine o'clock." This is all that needs to be said. Too much talk here is counter-productive. After the point is made, there can be a little small talk to reduce tension, and then the conversation can be ended. Don't fuss but don't get involved with excuses.

If the lateness continues, then you must go to Step 4 and ask, "What is your plan for solving this problem?" Here the manager is asking the employee to come up with something specific to take care of this situation that is costing the company money. Whatever plan the employee comes up with, as long as it is a bit beyond the simple statement "I'm going to be here on time, don't worry. From now on I'll be here on time," accept it. A simple plan might be: "Well, I think I have to get an earlier train or change the car pool." Whatever the employee says, accept it, but make sure something definite is planned. Make sure the employee becomes aware that there is a faulty behavior pattern involved that must be modified in order to correct the situation.

Having gone over the rules and elicited a plan, you should now ask for a definite time commitment to that plan. If the employee says, "I'll be here on time from now on," you should say, "Well, let's make 'from now on' a definite time. Let's see if for the next month you can get yourself here on time." If the employee is on time for the next month, you should ask him or her in and ask if the problem is solved. If the employee says it's solved, there is a good chance it is.

If after a few days the employee wants to talk more about the situation, it would be wise to listen. Here judgment comes in. You might wish to consider a special set of working conditions for this person, if it is possible to do so without disrupting the organization. This can sometimes work if the person is operating independently of others. By and large, however, you must beware of opening a floodgate of exceptions. Your best approach as a manager in most cases is to treat everyone the same when it comes to routine matters. You'll be amazed how quickly a department can begin to take pride in the fact that all their people are at work at 9:00 A.M. while other departments' are not.

Suppose the employee persists in coming to work late even though a plan and a commitment have been made. At this point, you must say very succinctly that the plan isn't working. Here it's up to the employee. If you have to make plan after plan to deal with lateness, you are fighting a losing battle. If the employee can't come on time, termination should be considered, the lateness should be carefully documented and the employee be made aware of it. Otherwise, unless the company is small, there may be no effective way to terminate the employee.

Where termination is not a viable option, as is so often the case, you may have to resort to what can be considered a childlike approach toward behavior change. Remember, you want the employee to come on time, you've tried many times and made many plans together, and they have all failed. You can't fire the employee. What can you do? Say to the employee in a kind and supportive way, "Let's take a look at what you are doing before you come to work on the mornings you are late. Maybe I can make a suggestion to help you." Insist that the problem can be solved. Insist that the employee must be at work on time. You might actually go step-by-step from the time the person sets the alarm the night before to when he or she steps in the door at work and see if the sequence of events can be made more efficient somewhere.

The approach may seem childish, but when you are dealing with an employee who consistently exhibits irresponsible behavior in regard to minor problems, and whom it is not possible to terminate, the only way is a step-by-step analysis of behavior during which you both look for ways to improve it. You may be able to come up with a creative solution, for example, "It's important that we get together to start the day." Perhaps the employee needs your recognition; a few minutes together at the beginning of each day may be enough to end the lateness. A good manager or supervisor might sense that for a short time this might be what the employee needs. Unfortunately, this type of solution makes the manager too much a part of the answer. The manager surely has better things to do than meet with this employee for ten minutes at nine o'clock each morning. It is, however, sometimes a way of getting started. Another radical suggestion might be to have a night worker at the office call the employee and wake him or her up. People with bad habits are stubborn, but a stubborn, creative manager can sometimes solve these "little" problems with out-of-the-ordinary methods.

Fortunately, most employees don't need to be treated this way, but for those who do, it's well to keep in mind that if you continue to allow someone who cannot be terminated to come to work late, and you don't take this detailed, step-by-step approach, your irritation will increase. You will tend to spend less time with the employee, criticize him or her more, argue, carp, get involved in excuses, and generally make your relationship so uncomfortable that the efficiencies of both will be impaired.

It's far better to be supportive and persistent. Don't be afraid to let employees suffer the natural consequences of their late behavior. Point out how behavior affects raises and promotions. Give them something to hope for in the future. Keep trying. Little problems often need more persistence than big ones; they can be solved if the parties like each other and are willing to try.

10

Dealing with the Alcoholic Employee

Almost every society has a drug that is used to relieve stress. In the affluent Western world, the main drug is alcohol. For thousands of years it has been used by people to make the intolerable tolerable, to make the frightening less frightening, to make the miserable less miserable, to make the lonely either feel that they have friends or that they don't need them. Used wisely in moderate amounts and at appropriate times, alcohol can be an excellent stress reliever; it is only the excessive and unwise use of alcohol .that gets people into trouble. Unfortunately, the boundary between moderation and addiction is not clear-cut, but there are some reliable guidelines.

Most heavy drinkers don't believe they are addicted. They deny emphatically that they have a problem with alcohol, even though they readily admit that once in a while they drink more than they should. They have a hundred excuses to explain why this happened one time, and they say they now have it under control, that you shouldn't worry about it, and that "everyone takes a few too many once in a while, so why make such a big deal about me?"

Only someone close to the alcoholic has a chance to recognize the problem, and only someone respected and needed by the alcoholic has a chance to do the initial counseling that can lead the alcoholic to seek help. It is the responsibility of managers who suspect a subordinate or co-worker is moving in the direction of alcoholism to take a stand and try to direct that person toward assistance as soon as possible. In this chapter we will emphasize what managers and supervisors can do. We realize that managers have neither the time nor the expertise to treat the problem of alcoholism, but they can be the first people to get the problem employee moving toward proper treatment.

There are four steps that managers and supervisors should take when they suspect that someone at work has a problem with alcohol that is affecting their performance.

1. KNOW WHAT RESOURCES ARE AVAILABLE TO THE PROBLEM DRINKER

Few, if any, alcoholics have been helped by one-to-one counseling, even with the most skilled counselor. Therefore, don't feel it's your job to get into a long, involved counseling situation with an alcoholic employee. Even if you had the time and the skill, your chances of success would be limited. The only successful programs for alcoholics are group programs. Your discussions with the alcoholic are only to direct him or her to some treatment group or to a company counselor who will be able to counsel more extensively.

Most large companies have counselors who are specialists in dealing with the problem of alcoholism. They have the expertise and knowledge to direct the employee toward the most suitable community resources and programs. They are also in a position to assist managers and supervisors in dealing with employees before, during, and after they avail themselves of help.

In the absence of such a company specialist, the manager and personnel department should be aware that the group most successful in treating alcoholics is Alcoholics Anonymous (AA). There are similar groups in many communities—hospitals, halfway houses, group therapy programs, group and individual psychotherapy programs—but unless you have an overwhelming number of alcoholic employees, you need only be aware that such a support system exists.

You should know specifically where your local AA chapters are and be in touch with several AA people to whom you can specifically refer the alcoholic worker. You might also find out what your company insurance program will pay for treating alcoholic employees and have on hand the name of at least one doctor who specializes in this kind of patient. If you have this minimal information, you are prepared to begin to help employees with this serious problem.

2. TALK WITH THE PROBLEM DRINKER
HONESTLY AND OPENLY

If, on the basis of poor performance, you suspect that an alcohol problem exists you should talk with the employee directly and quickly. How strongly you press depends on your company policy, but we advise companies to face their responsibility squarely. (If it turns out that the person is not an alcoholic, you can apologize and say you were worried. If you are right—and probably you will be— you may literally have saved a life.)

Call the alcoholic person to your office when there will be no interruptions. In a strong and compassionate way, try to get the person to recognize the problem. *Use the eight steps of RPM.* As much as the person may try to avoid facing the fact that he or she has a problem with alcohol, you must press. Do not be afraid to confront the employee with your belief that he or she is drinking too much if the person's performance is deteriorating. Expect denials, but don't give up easily. If there is ever a time to apply Step 8 of RPM, it's in working with alcoholics. Be prepared to spend at least 20 to 30 minutes once and maybe twice or three times with this employee.

In dealing with a suspected alcoholic employee who exhibits excessive absenteeism or whose output falls, a good question to ask is how much money he or she spends on alcohol: "What is your monthly liquor bill?" Ask the person, "Did you have a drink before breakfast or at breakfast?" Ask how many drinks he or she had for lunch today or yesterday. If the person continues to deny everything, the final check is to ask, in all sincerity, "Please think hard and tell me. In the past month, when did you ever stop after one drink?" Alcoholics can remain without a drink for a day, a week, or even a month; but once they've had one, they are compelled by the nature of their problem to take another and another and another. Therefore, if alcoholics can't answer this key question they may break down and admit their problem. If you have lunch with the employee, make a point of urging him or her, as a kind of joke, to stop after one drink. You may not have to do anything else; your point will be made. The person will recall what happened and may finally admit the problem when you talk the next time. Remember, say nothing more about the problem at lunch except to urge him or her to stop at one drink.

We believe that when dealing with alcoholic employees whose work record, even apart from their alcoholism, justifies termination, it should be company policy to go as far as to threaten them with termination if they don't stop drinking. The longer a person drinks, the less likely rehabilitation will be successful. The alcoholic who has not stopped drinking will become a burden not only to the company but also to his or her family, community, and society in general.

Don't believe that alcoholics don't know they have a problem. Alcoholics have excellent insight into almost every facet of their drinking problem. What they don't have is the strength to stop drinking. This is why they deny the problem so strongly. It is terribly painful to admit that you lack strength to control yourself. The tough manager or supervisor who, using the strengthening steps of RPM, confronts the alcoholic employee with the problem and then with the fact that there is help for the problem is the one who will help an alcoholic. Less than this simply won't work.

3. FOLLOW THE EMPLOYEE'S PROGRESS

Once the alcoholic gets involved in a helping program such as AA, make it your business to have brief follow-up talks at regular intervals, making sure the employee continues to attend the program. These talks may take only a few moments, or they may involve a little discussion about how things are now that the drinking has stopped. Be positive, supportive, and reinforcing of everything the employee is doing to stop drinking, but be especially supportive about the organization that is helping.

If the employee talks about quitting the program because the problem has been solved, don't stand for it. Rant, rave, threaten, turn handsprings, but don't let him or her quit. Push for continued participation. The employee probably won't make it alone, no matter how long he or she has gone without a drink.

4. GET THE ALCOHOLIC EMPLOYEE TO HELP YOU WITH OTHERS

Once the alcoholic has become rehabilitated (when he or she is working effectively, attending AA or some other organization, and continuing brief supportive follow-up counseling with you), ask for help with other employees who may have the same problem. This is the final and perhaps the key part of the rehabilitation. The ex-alcoholic in your organization is the best person to reach other employees in trouble.

The next time you run across someone whom you believe has a drinking problem, talk with him or her and then ask your rehabilitated alcoholic employee for some *concurrent* help. Rehabilitated alcoholics will be able to supplement your approach in a way that you can't. They've been there. They know all the tricks, the excuses, every twist in the road. They will quickly help you guide the present alcoholic toward a course of action that has a chance of success. This isn't foolproof. You must keep tabs on what is going on and make sure you are working together.

For the ex-drinker, this role really wraps things up. There is the satisfaction of having overcome the problem, but also the satisfaction of helping someone else. This gets the flywheel spinning fast in the right direction and makes the desire to drink more remote. Good managers, then, once they have dealt with an alcoholic successfully, have an ally or even a series of allies on whom they can and should call if this problem surfaces again.

These are simple steps. Keep them in mind. Read this chapter over several times before you counsel an alcoholic employee. Work hard to get your company to put teeth in its alcoholic counseling by threatening the employee with termination if he or she doesn't become involved in the program. Efforts that fall short of these guidelines are harmful to the company and disastrous to the employee.

Conclusion

In Part I we have discussed why some people move toward a success identity and others slip down the three stages of progressive failure. Review the chart in chapter 1 and see how all this makes sense in terms of employees who give up, employees who have symptoms, and employees who have negative addictions like alcohol or drugs. Think about the people you know at home and at work. Where do they fit in and why?

Occasionally reread the chapters that explain the eight RPM steps. As you read and understand them, you can correlate them with the information on the chart, in chapter 9, and in this chapter. You will become much more capable of dealing effectively with problem employees and others you know who are failing.

PART TWO

Both-Win Management

The American Management Association defines management as the art of getting work done through people. The process by which this is accomplished is through day-to-day negotiations between manager and employee.

The chapters that follow show why both-win negotiation is a logical and acceptable approach to management. Chapter 11 demonstrates that, as in any other negotiation, the success of the interaction is determined by how the parties deal with one another as human beings. Chapter 12 covers a number of management tactics that lead to harmonious agreements, while chapter 13 discusses the counterproductive tactics that push a relationship into disarray.

We believe that people have more power to change the direction of their organization than they think. Managers and supervisors are searching desperately for people who care. They are quick to recognize when employees are willing to give something of themselves to reach organization goals. Chapter 14 tells what employees at every level can do to enhance their authority or prestige.

The book ends with a prescription for success. The relationship between manager and employee will never again fit the do-it-or-else mold of yesteryear. Success in tomorrow's management world will be based on the human but performance-oriented approach of RPM.

11

Both-Win Management: How to Make Every Interaction and Assignment a Both-Win Situation

Negotiation has been called "the game of life." And so it is. We negotiate in everything we do from marriage to management and, of course, in buying and selling. The ideas of both-win negotiation in management are new. They could not have been implemented a few years ago. But in today's world of business, they must be put to work.

From the birth of the industrial revolution in the 1700s to the 1920s, there was one recognized and accepted technique that most managers used in dealing with employees: Take it or leave it. The theory was simple. The manager was paid to know what was needed and the employee was paid to do what he or she was told. In keeping with this approach, the emphasis in management was not on people but on methods. Efficiency was the main theme. Experts like Frank Gilbreath, the time-study genius, proved that organization of work was the key to improved productivity. American management from 1880 to 1920 became a model for the world.

By 1920 the times were changing. The United States came out of World War I as an industrial giant. There was prosperity, and jobs were plentiful. Human-relations theorists began to probe more deeply into what made people work effectively. They found out what the best managers already knew, that good human relations had a lot to do with motivation and job satisfaction. What followed was a rush of ideas on how to handle people, ranging from the traditional planning, organizing, staffing, directing, and controlling principles to such courses as "Management by Objectives," "I'm

OK, You're OK," "Time Management," "Decision-Making," and the "let it all hang out" Sensitivity Training with which some companies experimented in the 1960s.

Now is the time for all of us in business to recognize that management is indeed a negotiation, a process by which the manager and the employee exchange benefits for the purpose of gaining satisfaction. We live in a new kind of industrial world. Today's employee, from blue to white collar, demands and deserves a greater participation in managing and doing his or her own work.

THE BOTH-WIN APPROACH AND WHY IT WORKS

The ability of managers and supervisors to motivate employees depends not on their knowledge of theory but on the firing line of human relations. How managers handle employees in day-to-day dealings and how they negotiate a specific assignment can mean more than what they know about theory.

Before going into how to negotiate a both-win task assignment, we will first distinguish it from the older, "one-win" approach used for centuries. See the box opposite, titled "Characteristics of the Manager-Employee Relationship." Pay particular attention to the equations near the top of the table. On one side we show $5+5=13=(7+6)$; on the other we show $5+5=10=(8+2)$ or $(3+7)$ etc. How can $5+5=13$?

In a both-win relationship we *create economic value*. For example, imagine that you have asked a male employee to move a big desk from one room to another. It's a large desk, but he can do it by himself in about twenty minutes by pushing and pulling the desk around. The employee, instead of blindly doing the task, suggests that it may be wiser to assign an additional man to help for five minutes. Suppose you agree. Soon, two people working together finish a job that would have taken one person four times as long. We have created economic value through synergy and give-and-take. By working together we made $5+5=13$. Everybody wins.

There are other reasons that the new approach is better than the old. One-win is threatening, secretive, and self-centered. Both-win is participative and creative. Whereas the one-win approach is authoritarian, passive, and focuses on short-term problems, the both-

---

CHARACTERISTICS OF THE
MANAGER-EMPLOYEE RELATIONSHIP

(Both-Win)	(One-Win)
$5 + 5 = 13 = (7 + 6)$	$5 + 5 = 10 = (8 + 2)$ or $(3 + 7)$ etc.
Give-and-Take (Compromise)	Take (No Compromise)
Long-Term Relationship	Short-Term Relationship
Cooperative-Centered	Self-Centered
Open Communications	Secrecy
Opportunity-Oriented	Problem-Oriented
Participative	Authoritarian
Creative	Passive
Easing of Tensions	Tension-Producing
Non-Threatening	Threatening
Adult-to-Adult	Adult-to-Child
Builds Self-Responsibility	Builds Dependency

---

win approach emphasizes stable, long-term planning horizons and human relationships. Both-win is based on give-and-take; one-win is based on take it or leave it. We believe that the balance sheet clearly favors both-win management in today's work world.

PUTTING BOTH-WIN TO WORK ON A TYPICAL PROBLEM: THE EMPLOYEE WHOSE WORK IS SLIPSHOD

Administrative duties are about the same the world over. Almost every job requires the preparation of regular progress reports. The employee is generally required to collect and analyze data, to initiate some corrective action, and to "put out fires" when they arise. Furthermore, the employee is expected to protect the boss by serving as an early warning system, reporting potential problems before they get out of control.

Assume you are the manager of the budget department. You have five people below you, each of whom is responsible for a different area of cost control. You are having trouble with the person in charge of overhead cost, whose work tends to be slipshod. You call the overhead cost person into your office to negotiate a both-win plan for improving performance (RPM Step 4). You have the facts: The employee's weekly reports are generally late and the analysis is superficial; the reports rarely initiate corrective action, and potential problem areas have not been reported to you soon enough to avoid crisis. The employee appears to be working hard but doesn't seem to get much done.

Before negotiating a "get-well" plan with your employee, remember the essentials of a good plan:

1. The plan should benefit both parties.
2. The employee must participate in making the plan.
3. The employee usually knows more about the details of the job than the manager.
4. Regular follow-up is important.
5. Specificity is the key element. Specific targets, standards, task descriptions, milestones, and follow-up are necessary.

ELEVEN PAYOFF AREAS WHERE GIVE-AND-TAKE CAN MAKE A "GET-WELL" PLAN POSSIBLE

We have said that every task assignment can be changed so that both the manager and the employee benefit. Look at the Both-Win

---

BOTH-WIN NEGOTIATION CHECKLIST

1. When it's to be done
2. What is to be done (looking at the detailed work process)
3. Who does the job (dovetailing people to jobs)
4. Improved tools
5. Work inspection
6. Priorities
7. Personal incentive
8. Timing of change (how much, how fast)
9. Long-term procedures and policy
10. Learning the job
11. Organizational interface

Negotiation Checklist. You'll notice that there are eleven potential payoff areas, which are explained in detail below. The list is designed to help the manager and employee find a better deal for both parties in a systematic way. The cost control "get-well" performance plan can easily incorporate these give-and-take negotiating areas.

1. The "When It's to Be Done" Negotiation Area

Inherent in any task is the possibility that it can be scheduled differently. For example, it might be wise to require overhead reports every two weeks instead of every week but to have the travel account compiled weekly because it has gotten out of control. The time a job is to be done can be negotiated. There is usually a better time schedule that will suit both parties.

2. The "What Is to Be Done" Negotiation Area

If you want an area for negotiation which is sure to pay off, look at the details of *what* is being done. Follow the process carefully. You'll see work that must be done and some work that can be omitted. It may be that information or work which was once important to us no longer is. Time, usage, and technology always affect processes. There's a real payoff in looking at the work-flow process.

3. The "Who Does the Job" Negotiation Area

There are two aspects to this area: (a) the number of people who should help and (b) whether the talents of the person(s) doing the job dovetail with the requirements. With respect to the number of people, a manager can often improve performance by having more than one person do a task or, conversely, by having only one person do it.

With respect to the second aspect, different people are good at different things. Both-win management says that you fit round pegs into round holes. It's only common sense, but we've seen a lot of bad-fit situations that could have been avoided with a little creative thinking. The overhead cost control person who is performing badly may be better suited for accounts receivable. The employee with problems in cost may be perfect for an administrative position relating to office allocations or be better at maintaining surveillance over direct labor and materials.

4. The "Improved Tools" Negotiation Area

It's surprising how often a job is done with poor tools. All of us have had to add a lengthy column of figures without a calculator or have tried to loosen a screw with a screwdriver that was too small. At best it's frustrating; at worst it's costly. But there are many reasons why employees may not complain to you about poor working tools. Sometimes they feel that it's your problem, not theirs. At other times, the poor tools become an excuse for marginal performance. Your role as a manager or supervisor is to make certain that your employees have adequate access to such tools as a calculator, a secretary, timely incoming reports, and a copying machine. Don't wait for employees to complain; it's your job to be sure that they have the right tools.

5. The "Work Inspection" Negotiation Area

Inspection is a costly but necessary part of all work; it is risky never to inspect, but a full inspection is expensive and time-consuming. A better risk and cost balance usually results in a both-win situation. A good manager or supervisor will regularly check employees' work output but will consider the trade-off between 100 percent quality control and the acceptable level of statistical or partial control which is less expensive. The budget manager may be able to make everybody's life easier by looking at how much time is spent on perfectly typed and checked statistical reports and pretty charts. These may be eating away at employees' time, leaving them no time to do more important things. Inspection is necessary, but too much can be as costly as too little.

6. The "Priorities" Negotiation Area

Priorities planning pays off. The "90–10 Rule" says that 90 percent of all effort is directed at 10 percent of the payoff work. Employees spend most of their time doing work that does not bring in much revenue. It is easy to improve productivity and performance by changing the priority-effort balance. Managers and supervisors have a critical responsibility in this area. If they cannot get their priorities straight, the employees never will. Generally, employees must, for their own peace of mind, take things one at a time. The manager's role is to help put each task in a business perspective, so that priority conflicts can be surfaced and negotiated. Our accounting manager would be unwise to assume that the cost person is able to establish businesslike priorities on the work without direction. A great deal of coaching may be necessary before the cost person can see the total picture.

7. The "Personal Incentive" Negotiation Area

Everybody simultaneously works for his or her own personal incentive system as well as for the company. Time off, recognition, and peace of mind are just a few of the personal incentives that can lead to improved performance and "get-well" plans. There are many unspoken issues in the "personal" negotiation that takes place when manager and employee get together. That's where the eight steps of RPM can help you get to know the employees better.

8. The "Timing of Change" Negotiation Area

Improvement takes time. Not everything can or should be done at once. Setting reasonable goals is a good way to reduce the stress associated with making a change. For example, in the case of our overhead cost control person, it might be wise first to introduce changes that affect the timeliness of that employee's reports before trying to improve the quality of the analysis. The rule is: one problem at a time.

9. The "Long-Term Procedures" Negotiation Area

Some changes and improvements can best be made by changing procedures or policies. In large organizations, such changes take a long time, but if employees know that new policies are on the horizon it can help them do a better job today. It gives them something to look forward to and they know they have been heard. The problem of late reports and inadequate analysis may lie in systems and procedures and not with our cost control person. What may be necessary is a change in how accounting data, purchase requisitions, and paid bills are handled. What may be needed to control overhead costs is an early warning dollar commitment procedure that tracks big expenditures quickly and lets small ones be processed normally.

10. The "Learning the Job" Negotiation Area

If you want your employee to do a better job and to gain strength, you have to teach him or her. All learning takes work and time, and costs money, for both the learner and the teacher. Only too often a manager will pick on an employee for something the employee cannot change because he or she was never taught correctly in the first place. Managers who want employees to perform must give of themselves. They must take the time to teach workers to do the job properly. The employees, in turn, must make the effort to learn.

11. The "Organizational Interface" Negotiation Area

There is little we do that does not interface with others in our own business organization or in outside organizations. All of us have had the experience of being unable to accomplish something because of constraints set by superiors and others. The manager who recognizes this fact of life in planning has a better chance of handling it. Imagine once more that you are dealing with the cost control administrator. The organizational diagram below represents the various people with which each party must negotiate and coordinate before a change in performance can be made. The cost control administrator may *want* to get the report out faster and to do a better job, but he or she may be unable to do this because of others, who do not help or do not care. The manager may want to help the employee but be unable to because of other commitments. Managers and employees who are sensitive to constraints imposed by the organization have a better chance to improve performance on a both-win basis.

The following four points are good to remember when dealing with another party in the organization:

TYPICAL ORGANIZATIONAL CONSTRAINTS SURROUNDING MANAGERS AND EMPLOYEES IN DEALING WITH ONE ANOTHER

Top Management			Peers
Manager's boss			Accounting department
Controller			Computer department
Project managers			Different department heads
Sales			Subordinates
Engineering	Manager	Employee	Secretary
Peers			Operating executives
Other subordinates			Systems and procedures
Systems and pro- cedures			Other input/output people
Customers			
Purchasing			
Vendors			
Personnel			
Training			

1. Conflicts between departments and the people within them are inevitable. There are different goals, resources, and priorities.
2. Although many organizations may have inputs into a problem, only a few (perhaps only one) are decision-makers with respect to the problem. Look for the decision-maker.
3. One good measure of a manager's or employee's effectiveness is how well he or she can negotiate with those in the immediate organizational sphere of influence.
4. The manager's role is to help the cost control person negotiate more effectively within organizational relationships. The employee's role is to help the manager deal with those to whom he must answer.

The last point deserves special emphasis. A good manager or supervisor *helps* employees work harmoniously with others. The manager must not only introduce employees to the job carefully but also take the time to follow up on how they get along. It may seem to be a small point, but it will earn you the respect and appreciation of your employees.

Next time you have to deal with an employee or someone in another department who is difficult to work with, try drawing an organizational diagram like the one in the chart. It will give you an insight into the problem and how to solve it.

Conclusion

Both-Win Management is a new approach to dealing with people at work. It conceives of management as a negotiation involving considerable give-and-take. New managers will have to negotiate more than their older counterparts, but they will thereby gain greater acceptance and greater commitment from their employees.

12

Sixteen Both-Win Tactics Every Good Manager Can Use

There is a big difference between strategy and tactics. Strategy is knowing where you want to go and why. Tactics are the means by which you get where you're going. There are a lot of managers who try to get an employee to improve his or her performance without thinking through to the longer term ramifications. Lacking a strategy, such managers have little chance to succeed. They spend most of their time putting out fires and pushing people around.

Assume you have called an employee who is performing poorly into your office for a talk. Are you able to answer the following questions?

1. What specific performance improvement do you want to achieve from this meeting? What decision do you want the employee to make?
2. What do you want the employee to learn from this experience, and how do you hope the employee will benefit?
3. What are your long-term objectives with respect to the employee?

The strategy of Both-Win Management is to help the employee grow stronger and more self-responsible. Every encounter you have with the employee is designed to build confidence by moving him or her toward successful performance. We implement our strategy by applying the eight steps of RPM and negotiating a both-win interaction.

Tactics follow from strategy. The sixteen tactics we shall discuss are in no way manipulative. What they do is pave the way for a both-win, mutually satisfactory relationship between you and your employees. As you read these tactics, recognize that their purpose is to facilitate a better interpersonal negotiation at each of the eight RPM steps.

1. CONCESSION-MAKING: THE BEST WAY TO GIVE IN

All relationships in life are exchange processes, matters of give-and-take. If we want a person to change for the better, we must be prepared to give something of ourselves or something else the person values in order to get it.

A successful negotiation leaves both parties more satisfied than when they started. Managers should of course do all they can to leave employees with as much satisfaction as possible. Most people believe that the more concessions people get, the more satisfied they will be. We don't agree. We believe that *how* one makes concessions can be as important as how much is given.

The following rules of concession-making are designed to provide a high level of satisfaction to the other person:

A. People generally do not appreciate something they get too easily. Be helpful and friendly, but don't be afraid to ask for the performance you want. When you give in too easily or lower your standards too quickly, the other person feels that you never meant it in the first place and he or she doesn't appreciate the results.
B. Don't say yes or no too quickly. People respect a considered response more than one that is "shot from the hip."
C. Learn to ask for something in return when you make a concession. It puts a greater value on what you give, and besides, you might get what you ask for.
D. Don't be afraid to say no.
E. Give the other person a face-saving way out. Use RPM Step 4 to help the other person achieve dignity by working out a better plan. Instead of being burdened by bad performance, the person can be given hope for the future.
F. In general, with a strong employee it is likely that the more performance you ask for, the more you will get. With a weak em-

ployee you are better off setting performance targets that, although lower, are apt to be met. In that way you build strength through success.

2. WHERE TO TALK AND WHERE NOT TO TALK

When the Vietnam negotiations began, both sides discussed at great length where to negotiate. The Communists favored Poland, the United States wanted Hawaii. In the end, after months of dickering, a neutral site, Paris, was chosen. Both sides recognized the importance of where the negotiation took place.

The best place to have a meeting is in a quiet, friendly location away from the normal disturbances of work. This isn't always possible, so the next best place is your office or the employee's office. Do not allow any outside interruptions, whether phone calls or visitors. The meeting should take place where both of you can look at the facts and talk about them as privately and as comfortably as possible.

The worst place to discuss a problem is in front of others. There are few things more humiliating for a person than to be "chewed out" before friends and peers. If you want a big enemy, that's the way to make one. Other places to avoid are in the middle of the aisle, by the elevator, in the parking lot, and right on the work floor amid all the noise and traffic. Think of it this way. After years of marriage a man learns that certain subjects, like department store bills, should not be brought up while his wife is preparing dinner. To forget this is to pay a price at the table.

3. THE BEST TIME TO TALK

There are four times when it is wrong to discuss a performance problem with an employee:

A. When you have no time to work out a better way to do the job (Step 4 of RPM)
B. When you are angry

C. When the employee is in the middle of doing a job
D. When the employee is overwrought or emotionally upset over some personal or business problem

The best advice from the standpoint of time is to have regularly scheduled meetings with your employees. Next best is to set up a block of mutually agreeable time for getting together. Where and when to talk are particularly important in Steps 1, 2, and 4 of RPM. The time and place set the stage for progress and accord.

4. BACK UP YOUR FACTS AND GIVE A GOOD EXPLANATION

Managers should take the time to discover what the realities are. They should have available facts and figures supporting their position. Back-up information gives credibility and legitimacy to a manager's position. Back-up, especially in Step 2 of RPM, helps to keep the discussion from meandering into emotional channels. A good explanation makes it easier for people to change their positions, because it provides a face-saving rationale for change.

5. PATIENCE (NO QUICK DEALS)

Patience is the most powerful tactic of Both-Win Management negotiations. There is always a better deal for both parties if they take the time to search for it. Patience is a tactic all managers should learn. It brings out the full story; it separates assumptions from realities; it allows hidden alternatives to be discovered; it allows personal and organizational issues to surface. All this is impossible in a quick fix.

6. GRADUALISM

The employee who is performing badly will not improve in one day, so it makes no sense to expect it. The problem took a long time to develop, and it is likely to take a long time to correct. That's where gradualism can work for you.

Gradualism is a both-win tactic that pays off because it is a tool for resolving large differences in position. Sometimes the differences between two parties are so great that they cannot be bridged in one jump. Gradualism reduces the gap in small increments. Gradualism is a "peace-by-piece" tactic. For example, a sales manager believes that a reasonable sales target is $100,000 per month, while the salesperson believes that the $70,000 target is already quite high. They can agree to a plan that takes gradualism into account by setting the target at $70,000 a month for the next three months, $80,000 a month for the following three months, $90,000 a month for the next period, and so on.

7. "FOUR PARTNERS" MANAGEMENT

The "four partners" theory of management says that a comprehensive, intelligent plan can be worked out if the manager imagines there are four partners sitting behind the desk: the Past, the Present, the Near Future, and the Far Future. In their rush to take care of present problems, most people fail to consider the effects of their actions on the past and the future. Every new plan negotiated with an employee is linked to past relationships with that employee and with others. Any new plan is bound to affect the short- and long-term future. The intelligent manager will carefully consider and satisfy the needs of the four partners in dealing with an employee. This manager won't try to solve today's problem at the expense of tomorrow.

8. ACCEPTANCE TIME

It takes people time to get used to new ideas. Managers should recognize that employees may at first protest or otherwise be hostile to recognizing the realities of their present performance. Managers should allow time for employees to accept the new realities. It may take multiple sessions before an employee is willing to evaluate his or her present behavior honestly and participate in making a workable "get-well" plan as in Step 4 of RPM. Acceptance time is the bridge that carries people from marginal behavior to improved behavior.

9. AGENDA

Step 2 of RPM stresses sticking to the subject. All of us know how hard it is to keep any discussion on track, whether pleasant or not. When a supervisor confronts a subordinate with the need for improved performance, some emotional resistance is bound to arise. At that point, the discussion is apt to digress into useless recriminations.

The best way to minimize such digressions is to have an agenda. The manager should decide before meeting with the employee what will be discussed, the order of the discussion, and what will not be discussed. The subordinate should be made party to the agenda in any open way. Diplomats have long considered the agenda an essential tactic of negotiation. It is no less important in management relations.

10. WRITING DOWN WHAT YOU WANT

A good both-win tactic is for managers to write down what they want before meeting with an employee. From the manager's viewpoint, three self-directed questions should be addressed in writing:

A. What decision do I want the employee to make?
B. Why is the employee not making that decision?
C. What can I do to help the employee make the right decision?

The benefit of writing down what you want is that it forces you to negotiate with yourself in establishing priorities and classifying your needs. It forces you to separate realities from wishes. If you do not know specifically what behavior you want, you will have no chance to get it.

11. HOW TO BREAK A MANAGER-EMPLOYEE DEAD-LOCK

It's always harder to open a closed door than to open one that is slightly ajar. Never let the manager-employee relationship deteriorate to the point where neither of you can tolerate talking to the other. Here are some techniques for keeping the communication channel open:

A. Keep the discussion light. Don't take everything seriously. It's hard to be friendly in a grim atmosphere. A humorless tone is threatening.

B. Make changes in the work specifications. Go through the both-win negotiation areas in Chapter 11. You're bound to find some points that are mutually beneficial.

C. Change the time of discussion to a later date or change the place to a less threatening environment.

D. Change the time shape of uncertainty. That's a way of saying that both of you can reduce the risk of future trouble by taking certain precautions now.

E. Change the risk-sharing relationship. Instead of putting all the risk of failures on the employee, both of you might share it by doing some things together.

F. Bring a mediator into the discussion. When things get rough, you might consider having someone from personnel or a friend of both of you to cool down tempers. After all, this is what diplomats do.

G. Periodically write down points of agreements and points that are open to negotiation. This helps both parties realize that getting along is a matter of give-and-take.

H. Ask for time to gather more information. Never agree to something unless you have thought it through.

I. Make some concession. Often a small concession allows the other person to save face and breaks the ice.

J. Change the proposition or offer. Rephrase what you are proposing, or change it in some way. Never assume that the other person was listening carefully to what you said. Assume that they never heard a word (especially if the situation has strong emotional overtones).

Swallow your pride a bit more. The other person feels just as badly about the breakdown in communication as you do. Deadlock in human relations is hard to take.

12. CLEAR AGREEMENTS

Sam Goldwyn once said that a verbal agreement isn't worth the paper it was written on. A fuzzy plan falls into the same category. It generates loopholes and leads to deficient performance.

A specific plan is a clear plan. It leaves both parties with a positive "can-do" attitude. Clear, written agreements take longer to work out than fuzzy plans, but they are worth it. They help make the negotiated performance plan workable and reduce the likelihood of excuses or blame-laying later.

There is something comforting about having performance goals on paper. Both parties know what to expect. Would you have a plumber re-pipe your house without a meeting of the minds and a written agreement? There's a lot more at stake than that where your employees are concerned.

13. CONCESSIONS YOU CAN MAKE EVEN WHEN YOU CAN'T SAY YES

Give-and-take is essential to good interpersonal relations. The rigid person may win a few battles but is likely to lose in the long run. Most performance difficulties are amenable to compromise. They are rarely all-or-nothing, good-or-bad propositions. Here are some concessions that even the most rigid managers can make. They give nothing away but get a lot in return:

A. Listening
B. Giving a good explanation and honest information
C. Providing proof or evidence for statements you make
D. Making time for a long, undisturbed talk
E. Treating the other person nicely

F. Helping the other person make a decision
G. Smiling
H. Giving hope for the future
 I. Being consistent and reliable
 J. Giving recognition

14. NOTE-TAKING

An important part of the manager's job is teaching employees to be more effective. Good note-taking is critical. Take notes during the discussion and after it ends. Encourage your employee to do likewise. People forget what is said surprisingly soon. Notes help them remember.

15. LISTENING

The best and least expensive concession a manager or supervisor can make to an employee is to listen. Managers who listen will stand out and be well regarded. They will also be better informed. Listening expert Ralph Nichols says, "Immediately after the average person has listened to someone talk, he remembers only about half of what he has heard—no matter how carefully he thought he was listening."

Both-Win Management requires hard listening. It is too bad that most of us do not know how to listen. Listening is the easiest way to recognize needs and discover facts. If you take the time to listen, you can't help learning. The trouble is that you have to get out of some bad habits. For once you must look the speaker in the eye, be alert, sit up straight, get close, and be greedy to grasp new information. The employee will reward your efforts by making it easier to pick out the main points.

Why don't we listen? Of the eleven reasons given below, only the first is the responsibility of the speaker. The rest are self-inflicted impediments to good listening.

A. Most people speak before they think. Their speech is disorganized and hard to listen to.

B. We have a lot on our minds that cannot be switched off at a moment's notice.

C. We tend to talk and interrupt too much.

D. We are anxious to rebut the other person's arguments.

E. We dismiss much of what we hear as irrelevant or uninteresting.

F. We tend to avoid listening to hard material on the basis that it is too technical or detailed.

G. We allow ourselves to get distracted and don't concentrate; the distractions are more fun than the topic under discussion.

H. We jump to conclusions before all the evidence is in.

I. We try so hard to remember everything that the main points get lost.

J. We dismiss some statements because they come from people whom we don't consider important.

K. We tend to discard information we don't like.

A close look at the bad habits reveals that they center around one theme. Poor listeners permit themselves to drop out of the conversation in hopes of catching up later. Unfortunately they don't catch up.

Constructive listening begins with realizing that speakers are presenting themselves for your approval. They want you to see and believe their presentations. Like actors on a stage, they will perform better if you open your senses to what they are saying.

A person who speaks has a main theme, a few major supporting ideas, and proof that what is being said is sound. The trouble is that people don't follow that simple pattern. They mix things up. Anecdotes, ideas, irrelevancies, proof, and empty clichés are thrown together for the listener to unscramble.

How can we cope with this? We can ask the other person to summarize the main points and reasons. At times, we can do the summarizing and ask if our summary is correct. There is nothing wrong with saying, "I don't quite get the point" or "Let me get it straight. Do you mean to say . . ." or "I'm not quite sure how that ties in." The other person wants you to understand and will welcome the chance to make the point clear. You are doing the speaker a favor.

Listen actively. Listen as though you will have to summarize the main points to your boss. You will find that supporting details will fall into place if you get the main points. Make it a habit to repeat what has been said to the speaker so that he or she knows you understand.

Here are a few more listening tips that work every time:

A. Give your full attention. You can't listen and do something else at the same time.
B. Don't interrupt.
C. Discourage cute side remarks and distractions.
D. Don't cut off listening when something hard comes up.
E. Practice listening to ideas you don't like. Try to repeat what you've heard.
F. Let the other person have the last word.

Listening is the one concession managers can give that is guaranteed to get them more than they gave.

16. "THIS IS ALL I'VE GOT"

This very effective tactic can benefit both parties. An example of how it works in buying and selling will help show how to put it to work in management. A pool-builder proposes to build a pool for $10,000. The buyer looks over the specifications and responds that only $6,000 is available to spend. In effect, the buyer has said to the salesperson, "Please help me." If the buyer's appeal is credible, the seller's impulse will usually be to help by suggesting alternatives to meet the budget, such as variations in size, depth, payment terms, landscaping, equipment, and delivery time. These can help the buyer meet or come closer to the goal.

In the Both-Win Management variation of this tactic, a manager says to the employee, "This is what we have to accomplish. These are the only resources we've got to work with. What should we do?" This puts them into a both-win situation, because the employee becomes a partner in the solution. Just as salespeople generally know more about their products than buyers, so also employees usually know their jobs better than the boss. What this simple tactic does is focus the ingenuity of the employee on solving the difficulty.

Try it the next time your subordinate asks for six people in the budget when you only have funds for three. Watch how the discussion quickly moves to a both-win situation as you and your subordinate begin to develop alternatives. Ideas that neither of you considered before will come forth. The best part is that both of you will leave the meeting stronger. Each will have a better understanding of and commitment to the other.

Conclusion

If this were a book on business negotiation, the sixteen both-win tactics would be much the same. They are fundamental to productive dealings between people, whether the purpose is economic or social. RPM is, after all, a series of steps by which to negotiate a better human relationship. It is not surprising that these tactics, so effective in business, would also facilitate mutual satisfaction at work. In our next chapter we will look at ten tactics to avoid in business and in management.

13

Both-Lose Tactics Managers Should Avoid

We have pointed out that many managers and supervisors act in their own worst interests, handling people with what amount to "both-lose" tactics. Such unproductive tactics may be vestiges of unconscious habits that date back to times when workers feared for basic survival and settled for bare security. Many in authority who use them routinely today are probably unaware of the harm they are doing.

The RPM way is to be specific. In chapter 12 we were specific about the approaches that lead to a both-win exchange. In this chapter we will cover ten tactics that have no place in manager-employee relations. They are self-defeating for both parties.

1. "TAKE IT OR LEAVE IT"

The words "take it or leave it" have no place in good human relations. They always arouse hostility and cause the recipient to lose face by being backed into a corner. When freedom of choice is lost, a measure of self-respect goes with it.

At times it is important that an executive order be carried out quickly. For example, if a big job has to be shipped by 5:00 P.M. and it is 4:30 P.M., a manager might be justified in telling the shipping clerk precisely what has to be done rather than spend a half hour discussing the best way to do it. We recognize that emergencies arise and that assembly lines must be kept going, but we believe that too many assigned tasks leave no latitude for mutual give-and-take.

The trouble with "take it or leave it," even when those words are not explicitly used, is that they are top-down directed. They imply that knowledge is at the top and muscle at the bottom. In reality, those in charge rarely know as much about the job as those doing it every day. If a manager wants a job done, "take it or leave it" may work for a while. Indeed, for centuries it did work—with employees who were afraid to be fired. But if a manager wants a job done the best way, employee participation is necessary. "Take it or leave it" leads away from confidence and growth, not toward it.

2. "YOU GOTTA DO BETTER THAN THAT": THE KRUNCH

There are six magical words that work on salespeople and drive them crazy. They are "You gotta do better than that." "The krunch," as we call it in negotiation, doesn't deserve to work as well as it does. In the long term, we believe it creates more problems for the buyer than it alleviates. The same is true for the manager or supervisor who uses it when dealing with employees.

The trouble with "you gotta do better than that" is that it is too general. It preys on the insecurity of people. Most people recognize that their work has some flaws. The krunch puts the employee on the defensive without saying why.

But it is specificity that gets results. If you want improvement you must make a specific action plan to correct specific deficiencies. "You gotta do better than that" doesn't create solutions, only aggravations.

3. DEADLOCK

Deadlock is one of the most powerful tactics in negotiation. There is almost nothing that so tests the strength and resolve of an adversary. Most people avoid deadlock in business or social situations. They are afraid of it. Deadlock can be likened to alienation. One of people's greatest fears is that of being separated from others. People go to great lengths to avoid breaking valued relationships. Alienation from the boss has a traumatic effect on most workers. In the short run, they'll do almost anything the boss wants to avoid such a break.

Deliberate deadlock leaves a trail of resentment. A door once closed is harder to open than a door left ajar. Deliberate deadlock may have a place in negotiating, but it has no place in interpersonal affairs.

4. TOO-HIGH DEMANDS

In negotiation, the people who aim higher do better. Will a manager who sets higher performance goals with an employee get better results? It depends on how strong the employee is to start with. "Aim higher—do better" can be a dangerous philosophy in management. After all, the higher you aim the greater your risk of failure.

In general, we believe that a manager or supervisor can aim higher and get better results with employees who are already strong and competent. Such employees will strive to maintain the prescription for success. For marginal or incompetent employees, however, the rule is different. Aim at a performance level that is likely to assure success. For some employees this may mean a very low level, but that should not be the major concern. What we are trying to do is build strength and confidence. There is time enough to raise the demand for performance when the subordinate accomplishes the desired initial level of work.

5. THE BIG POT: REAL AND STRAW ISSUES

You should not use this tactic in management, but it works well for labor negotiations—so well that unions use it all the time. You will quickly recognize its impact from this old Russian story.

Once upon a time there was a wise man who lived in a Russian village. An unhappy woman came to him seeking advice. She lived in a small hut barely large enough for her husband and two children. It came to pass that hard times befell her husband's parents. They had no place to live. Being kind, she let them move into the already crowded hut. It soon got on her nerves. "What should I do?" she cried to the wise man.

He stroked his beard, thought awhile, and asked, "Have you a cow, dear lady?" "Yes," she said, "but what has this to do with my problem?" "I have an answer," he advised. "Take the cow into the hut for a week and then come back." She followed his advice reluctantly. After all, he had a good reputation as a wise man.

A week passed and things got worse. Every time the cow turned, the six occupants had to change seats. It was impossible to sleep. The lady returned to the wise man in tears. "I am more miserable than ever," she said and told him the whole story.

He stroked his beard, thought awhile, and asked, "Have you any chickens, dear lady?" "Yes," she said, "but what has that to do with my problem?" "I have an answer," he advised. "Take the chickens into the hut for a week and then come back." More skeptical than ever, she again took his advice, for he was the wise man.

A week later, hysterical, she returned. "You are insane," she said. "Your advice is bad. My hut is now impossible to live in. The cow turns, the chickens fly, the in-laws cough, the children find feathers in their soup, and I fight with my husband. It's all your fault."

He stroked his beard, thought awhile, and said, "Dear lady, try one more thing when you go home. Take out the cow. Come back in a week." "This man is a bit of a fool," she thought, but decided to follow his advice for the last time.

A week later she returned. "How do you feel, dear lady?" he asked. "This is ridiculous," she said, "but I feel a little better now that the cow is out of the hut."

He stroked his beard, thought awhile, and said, "I have a solution to your problem. Take out the chickens."

The lady took out the chickens and lived happily ever after with her husband, her children, and her in-laws.

That's the way the union uses the big-pot tactic against management. They create issues, some of which are real and some of which are made of straw. They do so to reduce management's aspirations and to give themselves trading room. When the company negotiator tells management that the union has agreed to remove the cows and chickens, everybody breathes a sigh of relief. It could have been worse.

The big-pot tactic may work in buy-sell or labor negotiations but we do not believe it has a place with employees. It clouds an already difficult situation with needless topics of argument. The rule for Both-Win Management ought to be: Keep it simple—keep it clear.

6. SURPRISES

One rule that managers and employees agree on is *No Surprises*. Employees don't want to think they are doing well, only to be clobbered at review time with a long list of complaints. Managers don't want to think that all is going smoothly, only to learn too late that things are falling apart. People can adjust to reality if given early warning, but they don't want to be surprised unless it's pleasant— and even that may have unforeseen consequences.

The Japanese surprised us at Pearl Harbor, but they lost the war. First, it got us scared, then it got us mad. Surprise has something going for it in war and perhaps in bargaining, but not in management.

The reason we don't like surprise is that it creates distrust and fear. It acts as a communication block. What worries us is that the introduction of unexpected events can cause employees to lose face and thereby harden their position or do something that puts the situation out of control. If either of these things happens, we are both in trouble.

7. FAIT ACCOMPLI: THE DEED IS DONE

The *fait accompli* (accomplished fact) is a tactic associated with diplomacy. It works as well in business. The principle is simple. Someone takes a surprise action designed to place him or her in a favorable negotiating position. The "accomplished fact" cannot help but affect the final outcome. India marches halfway through Pakistan, then negotiates. Had the negotiation taken place at the India-Pakistan border, results might have been different. It's a questionable tactic.

The saying "Possession is nine tenths of the law" is a familiar one. The action of taking physical possession has its own momentum. Action has a way of altering the balance of power. The strength of *fait accompli* rests in the fact that once a deed is done it is difficult to undo. In effect, the aggressor says, "I've done it. Now let's talk."

Does *fait accompli* take place in management? Yes. Managers often reorganize their departments or the work routine or promote people or move people from place to place without consulting them. Sometimes they ask an employee, "What do you think we ought to do?" when they have already made up their minds. Employees see through this approach and resent it.

8. GOOD GUY–BAD GUY

We have all seen "good guy–bad guy" tactics in the movies. A suspect is caught and interrogated. The first detective puts him under a glaring light, hits him with hard questions, and roughs him up. The tough guy leaves. In comes a nice man who shuts the light off, gives the suspect a cigarette, and lets him relax. Soon afterward, the suspect spills all he knows. "Good guy–bad guy" works better than it should.

How does "good guy–bad guy" work in negotiation? One person takes a tough stand, making large demands and acting in a contrary manner. Friendly old Smiley sits nearby and says little during the discussion. After a while the bad guy shuts up and the good guy takes over. Smiley's demands now seem reasonable by comparison. Why not? It's a pleasure to deal with such a nice person after being worked over by that mean one. You can't help feeling that things could have been worse.

"Good guy–bad guy" is a poor management tactic, although it is used frequently. Immediate supervisors, lacking the courage to confront employees with their poor performance, criticize them by saying that someone in a higher position is displeased. It's an unsettling tactic that employees soon see through.

9. ONE-UPMANSHIP

Employees get angry at managers or supervisors who try to get the upper hand by saying things that put the other party down:

A. "You're getting fat."
B. "You've been screwing up lately."

C. "You've made the same mistake ten times."
D. "You have a soup stain on your tie."
E. "I told you so. It didn't work, did it?"
F. "John does that a lot quicker than you do."

It's hard enough to deal with employees whose work is poor. Don't complicate it further by making them angry or putting them down. It may satisfy your ego, but it won't get the job done.

10. INVIDIOUS COMPARISONS

Some managers believe that people work best when they compete with their fellow workers. We don't think that is true. We believe that employees react badly to supervisors who create competition by making invidious comparisons between them. How would you like to have your spouse compare your salary to your neighbor's if yours were lower? Does such comparison lead to better performance, or will it move you toward a loss of confidence and self-esteem? Try not to compare the performance of one employee to another. If you must compare a poor performance to something else, compare it to some mutually acceptable level of productivity.

Competition between workers is productive only if it contributes to their psychological well-being and enhances the spin on their flywheels. When conditions can be created which allow two employees to compete on an equitable basis, competition may spur them on. However, a problem exists in most work situations: it is virtually impossible to compare many jobs in such a way that each worker can be given a fair handicap in running the race. Unless this can be done, competition is apt to be destructive rather than constructive.

Conclusion

The world of business and business negotiation can be tough. Some people perceive the manager-employee relationship in an adversary or competitive context, similar to the arm's-length dealings between buyers and sellers. Given such an orientation, it isn't surprising that they use whatever defensive and offensive measures are at their command. The manager-employee relationship, however, is not a battle between outside competitors. The measures that may be appropriate against outside forces are not appropriate if we want to make $5 + 5 = 13$ within our organization. For that reason we clearly differentiated the productive both-win tactics from those that lead to a both-lose situation.

14

How to Gain Power in Your Organization: The Subtleties of Authority and Influence

Management is a both-win negotiation. The manager wants to influence the employee in the direction of strength, effectiveness, and self-responsibility. The employee may want the same ends but may perceive the means to achieve them differently. He or she may see the job one way, while the manager sees it quite another way. They must negotiate. Each needs the other.

In this book, we have not yet talked of power, despite the fact that power is part and parcel of the outcome of every negotiation. In the last analysis, power exerts influence through its ability to control and allocate resources or benefits. Everybody knows that the boss has power and why. But, since almost everybody, manager or not, works for someone else, it's well for us to look at the power of those who want to influence the people they work for. We believe that employees have a lot more power and influence than they think. That's what this chapter is about: where the sources of influence and authority are in an organization and how to go about gaining them.

A common complaint these days is that people have so little control over their work lives. This complaint is especially prevalent among the younger, new breed of employees. Because these people became adults in a more liberated society, they expected that their voices would quickly be heard at decision-making levels. Now they feel like the caboose of a train. Decisions up front whipsaw those farther back in what appears to be a capricious fashion.

The wave of the future in management is to regard the manager-employee relationship as a both-win negotiation between partners. Notice that we have not said "equal partners," because in human relations and at work it is rare that two parties enjoy equal power. The successful relationship of the future will be based not on the traditional top-down power structure but on a more subtle interplay in which each party will exchange inducements and contributions to get the job done. They will be forced by the contributions to get the job done. They will be forced by the complexity of events to deal with one another in a contractual way, each having something to offer that the other needs.

We are not the first to view management as a both-win negotiation. The seeds go back to 1938, when the president of the New York Telephone Company, Chester Barnard, wrote a pioneering book on management. After a lifetime of business experience culminating as top executive of one of America's largest corporations, Barnard, a self-educated man, put his experience and thoughts in a book, *The Functions of the Executive*. In this book he raised three fundamental questions:

1. Where does the authority of an executive really come from?
2. What does an executive do?
3. What motivates an employee to work hard?

Chester Barnard had worked up from the bottom. His views were unique in that they combined a keen analytical mind with broad practical experience. His inducements-contributions theory of motivation was essentially a negotiation theory in which organizational inducements were exchanged for employee contributions.

It was when Chester Barnard questioned the basic source of a person's authority that he was most incisive and original. Barnard had seen authority from every rung of the ladder. He concluded that authority and influence did *not* stem from a person's position on the organization chart but was the result of other more subtle factors.

What are these subtle sources of influence in an organization? Listed below are ten ways to gain authority in your company, most of which Barnard recognized:

1. Get involved in planning
2. Demonstrate commitment and loyalty
3. Be competent, steady, and reliable
4. Be knowledgeable

5. Have self-discipline and self-control
6. Set a good example
7. Keep growing
8. Know the importance of coalitions
9. Get totally involved
10. Participate in drawing up procedures and making changes

Each of these sources of influence is a pathway toward greater control of one's own work world. Those who complain about their lack of influence might well consider these influence pressure points as avenues for *giving themselves* broader authority.

1. GET INVOLVED IN PLANNING

One of the best ways to understand and extend your control over events is to participate in the planning process at every level you can: for yourself, for your boss, for other departments, and, if possible, even in your customers' planning.

Planning is a hard job that many people avoid and most do poorly. People who are willing to get involved in advanced planning will see the forces at work shaping their destinies. They will, through their inputs to the plan, be better able to cope. Besides, planners always get an opportunity to talk to the boss, and that in itself will enhance your influence.

In another subtle way, planning can be an avenue by which employees can gain influence and authority, and that is through budgeting and scheduling activities. After all, a budget or schedule is a plan translated into dollars and time. These activities permit an alert employee to know where tomorrow's opportunities are likely to arise and to find a spot in the organization best fitted to his or her talents.

2. DEMONSTRATE COMMITMENT AND LOYALTY

There is authority in commitment and loyalty. People who are loyal to the organization and committed to its budgets, plans, schedules, and philosophy carry influence. Look at the influence of small, dedicated groups, which often have meager resources, in shaping our society.

One has only to look at the industrial might of the Japanese to see how important a part commitment and loyalty play. The people who work for a Japanese corporation are intensely committed to it. They demand from themselves the best work they can do, and they expect the same degree of self-responsibility from others. The Japanese have succeeded in translating the subtle power of the individual's commitment and loyalty to the company into what is now one of the strongest industrial nations in the world.

3. BE COMPETENT, STEADY, AND RELIABLE

People who are competent, steady, and reliable carry great weight in their organizations. In the age of "future shock," when people are jumping from company to company, job to job, and family to family, those who don't jump around are going to carry more influence in the decision-making process.

The trouble with steady and reliable competence is that it is not glamorous. But in the world of the future it is less likely that managers will take such values for granted.

4. BE KNOWLEDGEABLE

Sir Francis Bacon, Peter Drucker, and Chester Barnard shared the viewpoint that knowledge is power. It doesn't take a young person long to learn that certain people have great influence in the organization even when they are not high on the organization chart.

People who know their jobs are heard. Those who know how things really work inside the company contribute to policy and are listened to. People who have special areas of interest or know-how in addition to their direct jobs are usually the ones first considered for promotions. Those who know what is going on outside the organization are also in a good position to influence others in higher positions.

5. HAVE SELF-DISCIPLINE AND SELF-CONTROL

Self-disciplined and self-controlled people are respected. They serve as quiet models of what the rest of us could be if we could only get it all together. Well-organized people who use their time well, who can do several jobs at once, who can work and play and have time for their families, and who can live within a budget or a plan are in a position to influence events no matter where or at what level they work. Besides that, they usually feel good about themselves, and that helps them win respect from others.

6. SET A GOOD EXAMPLE

People who set a good example carry more authority and influence than those who do not. If you want people to do as you say, you must set a good example. Managers who want employees to maintain high levels of performance must do the same. They cannot continue to break their own rules.

7. KEEP GROWING

People who are learning and enlarging their perspectives carry influence. Those whose horizons include what is going on in the news, in the marketplace, and in the world of ideas, books, and theater are listened to. They are able to put the events that affect them into a broader perspective. Most people cannot or will not take the time to do this, and that is a big advantage to the person who remains curious and open-minded.

8. KNOW THE IMPORTANCE OF COALITIONS

The real power in organizations lies not so much in the individual but in coalitions of people. Loners, even competent ones, rarely carry the influence that *groups* of men and women do. The influence of the group lies in its ability to satisfy, through the negotiation process, the diverse interests of many.

Small-group studies and research into the informal organization indicates that group forces shape values, norms, and productivity in ways the time-and-motion experts never dreamed of.

9. GET TOTALLY INVOLVED

How very important this is. If you want to carry weight in your organization, it's easier than you think. *Just begin thinking like an owner.* Look at everything you do as though you owned the company. Understand not just *what* to do but *why* it's being done and *who* your customer really is. Get involved in your job whether you are the sweeper or the president. Know what happens to your work and how what you and others do relates to company profits and costs.

The magic of what we are saying is that regardless of your present level you'll be quickly recognized. *Involvement* is what those who pay you are looking for. Most people don't want to put themselves out to get involved. They say, "I'm not paid for that, the boss is. Let the boss do it, and I'll do the job *I'm* paid for." The few who do get involved carry great influence because there are so many who don't. Managers are smart enough to delegate authority and responsibility to those who think and act like bosses. Wouldn't you?

There is another power dimension of involvement. People who are involved with others, who care, who help, who mix, who volunteer, who work together, who interact at different work, play, and social levels, and who join in all these gain influence as well.

10. PARTICIPATE IN DRAWING UP PROCEDURES AND MAKING CHANGES

How often do people complain of stupid, restrictive procedures, only to learn that they had a hand in how they were written! Actually, the process of developing a new system is usually a relatively democratic one. People are given a chance to say what they think and later have a chance to discuss each point before the final sign-off.

If you want to exert more influence in your organization, participate actively in the procedure process. Too many people try to avoid the work and conflict involved in surfacing their viewpoints early. Instead they say, "The heck with it. We'll worry about it later." And later they do worry.

Conclusion

For those who complain that their voices are not being heard, we have suggested ten ways to enhance their authority. Employees who build their influence on these new pathways to power will find themselves making a better both-win deal with their managers. They will be negotiating from strength and mutual respect.

It would be naive to say that position on the organizational ladder doesn't matter. It does. The person who pays the piper has a lot to do with the tune, but not nearly as much as used to be.

You have more influence than you think.

15

Prescription for Success: The Manager-Employee Survival Kit

Any manager, from the company president down to the lead man, can use Both-Win Management to deal with the performance and personal problems that are part of every manager's job. In this book we have shown how to handle these time-consuming and costly matters so that they are less likely to happen again. We have demonstrated that RPM is an approach to manager-employee relations that teaches employees what to do so that they can correct their own performances in the future and thereby become increasingly productive, responsible, and self-reliant.

RPM Both-Win Management rests on certain premises about human beings at work. We call it "Theory RPM":

- It is people and performance problems that make the manager's job hard, not the technical aspects.
- Improved performance is a both-win proposition. Performance is important to the company, and it is just as important to employees in terms of their psychological strength and well-being.
- A person's behavior can be changed for the better if certain steps are followed and certain common pitfalls avoided. The eight steps of RPM can serve as a practical guide in helping people to improve their behavior.
- People want to improve if the climate is right. Good performance makes them feel good. Poor performance gives them pain. Feeling good about yourself is a powerful built-in motivator pointing in the right direction.
- People need involvement with others. They want to participate. They want a measure of control over what happens to them.

- From a performance-management (or behavior-change) standpoint, the manager is better off starting with people as they are *right now*. Why they are the way they are is less important than getting their flywheels going immediately.

Employees at all organizational levels will increasingly want more from work than salary and fringe benefits. With the advent of greater affluence and education, they will demand attention to their individual motivation reference levels. They will be disposed to negotiate rather than merely take orders. Like it or not, the trend is toward negotiated management, where the manager and employee work out a both-win action plan and live by it.

THE MANAGER-EMPLOYEE SURVIVAL KIT

What every manager wants are employees who solve problems, not make them. He wants productive, happy employees who are self-responsible, who make their own decisions, who do good work, who meet the negotiated objectives, and who are involved enough to care about the organization's well-being. This book has an arsenal of techniques for helping employees to achieve a success identity and for helping them become self-reliant, strong, and effective.

Here now are eighteen rules in the manager-employee survival kit. Managers who learn to apply them in their day-to-day contacts with employees will find the supervisory job easier and less frustrating.

1. Don't harp on past mistakes. A discussion of the past doesn't change the past. It only reinforces failure and raises the probability of future mistakes. The way to change performance for the better is to start with what is *now*.
2. Remember the rules about constructive criticism:
   Don'ts
   A. Don't criticize anything that cannot be changed.
   B. Don't criticize past mistakes.
   C. Don't hurt the other person in subtle or obvious ways.
   Dos
   A. Do show the other person the right way.
   B. Do build from strength.

   C. Do remember that people usually criticize themselves (perhaps too much).
   D. Do remember that people recognize and are sensitive to their own mistakes.
   E. Do remember that people want to learn a better way from someone who genuinely wants to help them.
3. After getting the facts and establishing the "now" behavior, let the employee self-evaluate whether his or her behavior is helping or hurting.
4. Don't get bogged down in emotions and "How did you feel?" discussions. Listen to an employee's feelings, but don't try to elicit feelings. The way to help people feel better is by moving toward performance.
5. Negotiate both-win performance plans with employees. Let them develop their own "get-well" plans as much as possible. Then tie it down through the give-and-take of negotiation.
6. Make sure that all plans are specific. Specificity leads to action, generalities lead nowhere.
   A. Be specific about what is to be done.
   B. Be specific about when it is to be done.
   C. Be specific about quality and quantity standards.
   D. Be specific about review points (milestones).
7. Encourage a strong commitment to the "get-well" plan. The greater the commitment, the more likely it is that the plan will be executed. No commitment = No performance.
8. Learn to give recognition when it is earned, but do it in the best way. Don't just say, "Congratulations, you did a good job." Instead, be specific.
   A. Ask the employee, "How did you do it?"
   B. Let the employee describe fully what he or she is most proud of.
   C. Give specific praise along the way.
9. Don't accept excuses. When you accept excuses for nonperformance you weaken people. When you move them toward performance you strengthen them. Move to action. Instead of talking about why it could not be done, develop a plan to do it right.
10. Never hurt, demean, or be punitive toward people. Hurting people does not teach them a better way, it reduces their confi-

dence and leads toward a failure identity rather than a success identity. It slows their flywheel down. Some ways in which managers hurt or demean employees are:

A. Talking behind their backs.

B. Ridiculing them.

C. Discussing their inadequacies with others.

D. Paying no attention to them or their suggestions.

E. Berating them in front of others.

F. Punishing them with demeaning special assignments.

G. Encouraging them to try, then clobbering them when they fail.

11. Allow people to suffer the natural consequences of their actions and decisions. Protecting people from natural consequences weakens them. It reduces their ability to cope in the future. When people suffer the natural consequences of their performance, they learn to be more rationally motivated the next time; that builds strength (provided the natural consequences don't foreclose the future altogether).

12. Strength builds strength. Performance leads to more performance. The best foundation from which to build future performance improvement is from successful performance. Just as it is bad to harp on past mistakes, it is good to search for and emphasize past positive accomplishments.

13. Always offer some hope for the future. People can get better if they have something to look forward to.

14. Don't respond to hostility with hostility. Hostility is best handled by

A. Being honest.

B. Avoiding a discussion of past mistakes.

C. Reviewing performance against the plan early enough to take corrective action.

D. Moving the discussion to "What can we do to make you feel better?"

15. Building rapport and goodwill with an employee or anyone else is a long-term affair. Aside from dealing with people in an honest, forthright, listening way, it is well to remember one crucial point: Don't destroy rapport by overreacting to a problem. Goodwill and trust take a long time to build and only moments to destroy. Learn to count to one hundred.

16. Be ready and willing to renegotiate a new "get-well" plan if the prior one fails. Don't give up easily. Employees will interpret your willingness to stay with them as a vote of confidence, and they will try harder.
17. There is always a better way to do a job. There is a better way for the manager and the employee at the same time. All we have to do is look for the both-win better way, and we will find it.
18. You have more influence and authority in your organization than you think. Think and act like a manager and you'll be respected like one.

Conclusion

The discerning manager will see that the ideas and practice of Both-Win Management are fundamental to any relationship in which we want to help the other person become stronger, more effective, and self-reliant. The eight steps of RPM, the ideas of both-win performance negotiation, the success-failure identity model, and the flywheel theory apply to those we work with, those we live with, and, of course, to ourselves.

Put RPM to work in your daily relationships. It will help those you work with, and those you love, to live fuller, more successful lives. It will get their flywheels going as well as your own.

Index

ABOUT THE AUTHORS

Chester L. Karrass, known to thousands of business executives throughout the country as "Mr. Negotiator," is Director of Karrass Seminars, which specializes in presenting negotiation, management, and sales seminars on a personal and video format basis. Over 130 Fortune 500 companies, including General Motors, General Electric, ITT, and Mobil, presently license his video program for their in-house use, and more sales, purchasing, and contracts executives now attend Dr. Karrass's negotiating seminars than all other negotiating programs combined.

An engineering graduate with a master's degree from Columbia University and a doctorate in Business Administration from the University of Southern California, Chester Karrass was the first recipient of a Howard Hughes Doctoral Fellowship in Business Management. The author of two highly regarded books, *The Negotiating Game* and *Give and Take,* he lives with his wife and two children in Bel Air, a suburb of Los Angeles.

William Glasser, M.D., is one of America's leading psychiatrists. A much sought-after lecturer both here and abroad, he is the founder of the Institute for Reality Therapy and the Educator Training Center and the author of five best-selling books, including *Reality Therapy, The Identity Society,* and *Positive Addiction.* An expert in motivational psychology, he has worked extensively with schools, and his concept of reality therapy has been applied to a wide variety of problems ranging from child rearing to industrial management.

Dr. Glasser received both a medical degree and a master's degree in psychology from Western Reserve Medical School and has studied psychiatry at UCLA and Veterans Administration Hospital in Los Angeles. He resides with his wife and three children in Brentwood, a suburb of Los Angeles.